Road Trip

Road Trip

True Travel Across America

Edited by Andrew Hoegl

St. Martin's Press
New York

This book is dedicated

to Dan "The Worm" Mirman

Designed by Jaye Zimet.

Library of Congress Cataloging-in-Publication Data
Road trip / Andrew Hoegl, editor.
    p. cm.
   Based on the Chrysler Corporation infomercial.
   ISBN 0-312-11137-1 (pbk.)
   1. United States—Description and travel.
 2. Automobile travel—United States. 3. Popular culture—United States. I. Hoegl, Andrew.
II. Chrysler Corporation.
E169.04R6   1994
917.304'929—dc20   94-6053
                        CIP

First Edition: December 1994

10 9 8 7 6 5 4 3 2 1

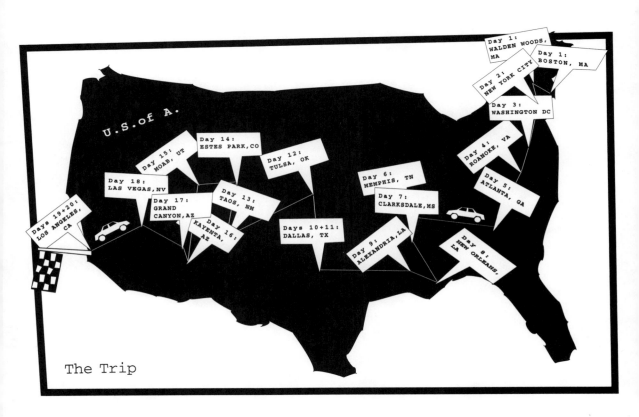

The Trip

Contents

SAM JONES

Road Trip is not your typical book in any sense of tradition. This is a book developed from a product-sponsored television program. The conversations herein were picked up verbatim from the videotapes that were made of this entire trip. They have been edited down considerably to include what we feel is the true essence, or the basic reality, of what was happening in the minds of these four individuals as they traveled for these twenty days across America. Excerpts from Cheri's diary (Cheri being one of the participants) have been included throughout the book and appear in the black boxes in the margins. At the beginning of each day, there are listings of various places of interest, places to eat, nightlife, and accommodations, plus mileage and raw drive time. Their purpose is twofold: They are useful if you happen to be in the area, and they provide the backdrop to where these conversations occurred.

9/6

Mr. Jim Fitzgerald
Executive Editor
St. Martin's Press
175 5th Avenue
New York, NY 10010

Dear Mr. Fitzgerald,

I am currently working as a segment producer on a one-hour, prime-time television
special called "Road Trip." The reality-
based show follows the experiences of four
young people who will take the ultimate
road trip across America this fall. Beginning in Boston, four "twenty-something"
strangers will drive across the country for
three weeks, seeing and doing as much as
they can cram into their schedule. The
travelers will not be actors, but real people selected from a nationwide search. We
will not script the show, but rather docu-
ment their trip on tape. There will be cameras in their car as well as field crews to
follow them as they explore America.

CHRYSLER CORPORATION

I am writing to you because I feel there is
potential for an interesting companion book
to this show. While researching the potential stops for our cast, I've talked with
many booksellers who indicated a dearth of
travel material for this demographic. I see
a product that will not only provide a useful travel guide, but will allow the reader
to live with our cast during their three-
week journey.

If you are interested in publishing this book, please contact me at the offices of Slam Dunk Productions.

Sincerely,

Andrew Hoegl
Freewheelin' Films/Slam Dunk Productions

Part 1

Getting Ready to Roll

GROUND 0:

Saturday, September 25:

Boston Interviews

Today is dedicated to preliminary interviews with the cast. Kurt and J.D. will take Craig and Mitch with them to each interview site. Dr. Pain and Sandie will spend the day rigging the interior of the car, Neon. There's still plenty to do, so everyone else should spend the day tying up loose ends.

PRODUCTION SCHEDULE:

8:00 A.M.–11:00 A.M.: Shoot first interview with Wade outside Firehouse.

11:00 A.M.–12:00 P.M.: Lunch and travel to second interview site.

12:00 P.M.–2:00 P.M.: Shoot second interview with Eileen at Boston College. (Are we cleared to shoot there?)

2:00 P.M.–3:00 P.M.: Travel to third interview and setup.

3:00 P.M.–5:00 P.M.: Shoot third interview with Cheri in business district. (Do we have a rooftop?)

5:00 P.M.–6:00 P.M.: Travel to fourth interview site and setup.

6:00 P.M.–8:00 P.M.: Shoot fourth interview with Brad. We need a site for this one, guys. Lake?

9:00 P.M.–?:00: Production meeting.

Production notes: We need someone to get each kid to their interview site on time!

The cast and crew of *Road Trip:* (Top row, L-R) Wade, Brad, Tiffany "Mother" Hoss, J. D. "Red Leader" Roth, Jeff "B. J." Werner, Jeff "Twist" Thisted, Tim "Dr. Pain" Smith, Craig "Sparky" Spirko, Kurt "The Mule" Brendlinger, Mitch "Ears" Pietz; (bottom row) Jonathan "Daredevil" Rho, Andrew Hoegl, Eileen, Cheri, Sandy Hauf, Eyde "What?" Belasco. SAM JONES

TO: All Crew
FROM: J.D. and Kurt
RE: Everything

Welcome to Boston!!! We just thought we should let you know what's happening . . .

All of you will receive your per diem on a weekly basis. So far you have received per diem until October 2. You will receive your next week's per diem then.

Per diem will cover all of your meals and incidentals. This includes phone calls at the hotels.

Unfortunately, due to the budget, we will have to double up in some instances including here, New York and others. We will try to get you guys singles wherever we can.

When you check into a hotel, please use a credit card for your incidentals. Room and tax will be covered.

The grip truck is for all equipment and personal bags. Please try to keep the motor homes clear of everything except for your carry-ons.

We will have two motor homes on the trip. One will become the control room and have video playback. The press will also conduct their interviews from there. The other is strictly for relaxing. We will dedicate that motor home as a hangout for the camera and sound guys.

Safety is an important factor. We advise that everyone remain seated in the motor

homes. We also advise seatbelts. There is
an emergency medical kit located on the
crew motor home. It is full of Band-Aids,
ointments, etc.

We need to keep contact with the cast to a
minimum. Any questions that are asked of
you in regard to the schedule or anything
about the show should be directed to J.D.
or Kurt. "Hi's" and "How are you's" are
okay, but try to keep it limited to that.

The schedule you have been given is a
framework for the trip. It will give you an
idea of where we are headed and at what
time. These days are extremely long, so use
drive time to rest up.

Any questions . . . ?

Brad Gober. SAM JONES

MEET THE CAST

NAME: **Brad Gober**

HOMETOWN: Cornelia, Georgia

AGE: 21

OCCUPATION: Student/Waiter

AMBITIONS:
To be Attorney General of Georgia

FAVORITE BOOKS:
The Art of War by Sun Tzu, *To Kill a Mockingbird* by Harper Lee

FAVORITE MOVIES:
Roots, Gone With the Wind

FAVORITE BANDS:
U2, Aerosmith, Ice Cube, Public Enemy, Janet Jackson

TURN-OFFS:
Ignorant, judgmental, closed-minded, insecure people

TURN-ONS:
Intelligence, confidence, vision, enthusiasm, perseverance

BEST GIFT YOU EVER RECEIVED:
The gift of love from my parents. They've been the greatest thing in my life. My whole family, really. I love being born a Gober.

THE HUMAN BEING YOU MOST ADMIRE:
Lafayette Gober. He's given me all the values that I have. A lot of my friends have

given in to drugs, etc. He's given me the
drive to be something better.

THE HUMAN BEING YOU MOST DESPISE:
Connie Sayer. Ex-girlfriend Laurie's
mother. Laurie is white and her mom made
her break up with me because I'm black.

YOUR GREATEST FEAR:
Not living up to my potential. I feel like I
am right now, but if something would hinder
me, I would drift off into nothingness.

FAVORITE RECREATION:
Tae kwon do. It's like chess. You have to
think while you're fighting. You have to be
physical, but it's a thinking man's sport.

YOUR LEAST FAVORITE PART OF YOUR BODY:
My legs.

BIGGEST PROBLEM FACING YOU TODAY:
Focusing on my goals and not being
distracted by everyday temptations.

HOW YOU FEEL ABOUT YOUR PARENTS:
I love them.

THE BEATLE YOU IDENTIFY WITH MOST:
Ringo. He's still going strong, still doing
what he loves to do.

HAVE YOU EVER STOLEN ANYTHING:
Other than a young girl's heart? No.

YOUR MOTTO:
I have two: (1) "Be about the business of
taking care of business." (2) "There's no
greater glory than to take a bullet for the
Georgia State Patrol. God has put no
greater man on Earth than a man who will

take a bullet for the Georgia State Patrol.
But mind you, when you take that one
bullet, you give that son of a bitch two."
That's by Two-gun Dunn, Captain, GSP,
retired.

Cheri Barr. SAM JONES

NAME: **Cheri Barr**

HOMETOWN: St. Louis, Missouri

AGE: 24

OCCUPATION: Waitress

AMBITIONS:
I'd like to be a travel director, guiding
tours all over the world for a year or so.
Then I want to go to law school.

FAVORITE BOOKS:
The Shining by Stephen King, *Of Mice and
Men* by John Steinbeck

FAVORITE MOVIES:
*The Jagged Edge, White Knights, The Music
Box, National Lampoon's Vacation*

FAVORITE BANDS:
New Order, Fleetwood Mac, Pearl Jam,
Erasure, Blondie

TURN-OFFS:
People who are stingy. I used to be really
stingy and I hated myself for it. Also,
know-it-alls. It's usually a sign of a lack
of intelligence.

TURN-ONS:
Hard bodies, long hair, goatees, confidence,
people with direction.

BEST GIFT YOU EVER RECEIVED:
Bail, for high school graduation. Some cops
broke up a party and I was put in jail for
assaulting a police officer and resisting
arrest. My parents bailed me out and that
was my present.

THE HUMAN BEING YOU MOST ADMIRE:
Maya Angelou, America's Poet Laureate, who
read at Clinton's inauguration. She seems
to have a grasp on what's important in life
and what's not.

THE HUMAN BEING YOU MOST DESPISE:
This girl, Shannon. She's the epitome of a
dumb blonde. I don't respect girls who act
dumb to get their way.

YOUR GREATEST FEAR:
Not being successful. I'm kind of in a lull
right now. I have the ability and knowledge
to be successful, but I'm not using it.

FAVORITE RECREATION:
Playing soccer. It's rough. I get pumped.

YOUR LEAST FAVORITE PART OF YOUR BODY:
My nose.

BIGGEST PROBLEM FACING YOU TODAY:
Finding a home. I'm getting kicked out of
my apartment by my roommates. They're
intolerant of my hours. I'm too loud.

HOW YOU FEEL ABOUT YOUR PARENTS:
I get along with them great. They said I
could go back and live with them. It's a
combination Cleaver/Bundy household.

THE BEATLE YOU IDENTIFY WITH MOST:
The Japanese beetle.

HAVE YOU EVER STOLEN ANYTHING:
I steal souvenirs from guys. Once I got the coolest pair of Vuarnet shorts.

YOUR MOTTO:
"You never get a second chance."

Wade Blackburn. SAM JONES

NAME: **Wade Blackburn**

HOMETOWN: Portland, Oregon

AGE: 27

OCCUPATION: Personal Fitness Instructor

AMBITIONS:
I want to get into the fire department. Before that, though, I want to try modeling in Milan or Japan and travel for a while. Basically, I want to be happy.

FAVORITE BOOKS:
Sacred Journey of the Peaceful Warrior by Dan Millman, *The Prophet* by Kahlil Gibran

FAVORITE MOVIES:
The Natural, Dances with Wolves, True Romance, Dead Poets Society, Singles

FAVORITE BANDS:
Enya, P.M. Dawn, Guy, Stone Temple Pilots, Caterwaal, The Eagles

TURN-OFFS:
Phoniness, people who aren't genuine. I can spot them in a second.

TURN-ONS:
People who are genuine and funny. People who don't judge you. Eyes. Smile. Legs.

BEST GIFT YOU EVER RECEIVED:
My BMX bike when I was ten years old. My
stepdad got it from a kid down the street.
It was one of the first ones with shocks on
the front. He painted it and fixed it up for
me and gave it to me for Christmas.

THE HUMAN BEING YOU MOST ADMIRE:
My mother. She's a very strong person.
She's been through so much. She had me when
she was seventeen and raised me and my
brother by herself. Also my brother,
because he never listens to anything I have
to say.

THE HUMAN BEING YOU MOST DESPISE:
My father. He was never around when we were
growing up, but still expects us to have
some kind of "Brady Bunch" attitude about
him.

YOUR GREATEST FEAR:
Not being successful. Not being happy with
what I'm doing and who I am.

FAVORITE RECREATION:
Any kind of sport. Mountain biking, water
sports, jet-skiing.

YOUR LEAST FAVORITE PART OF YOUR BODY:
My hands. My fingers are really skinny. I
don't like that.

BIGGEST PROBLEM FACING YOU TODAY:
Staying focused on what I want out of life.
I tend to wander and get distracted. I want
stuff now and it's hard to be patient.

HOW YOU FEEL ABOUT YOUR PARENTS:
My mom is always there for me; she's really
played both roles. My dad was never around.

I don't really know him and he doesn't really know me.

THE BEATLE YOU IDENTIFY WITH MOST:
I never really got into the Beatles.

HAVE YOU EVER STOLEN ANYTHING:
Yeah. Candy when I was real young.

YOUR MOTTO:
"What goes around comes around." I think if you're a good person it comes back to you. And if you're not, it still comes back to you.

Eileen Chung. EILEEN CHUNG

NAME: **Eileen Chung**

HOMETOWN: Rivervale, New Jersey

AGE: 20

OCCUPATION: Student

AMBITIONS:
I would love to be a photographer, but I think I'll go into advertising or marketing where I can incorporate photography.

FAVORITE BOOKS:
The Firm by John Grisham, *Where the Wild Things Are* by Maurice Sendak, *The Great Gatsby* by F. Scott Fitzgerald

FAVORITE MOVIES:
Dead Poets Society, A Few Good Men, Dirty Rotten Scoundrels

FAVORITE BANDS:
Depeche Mode, U2, The Sundays, Gin Blossoms, Billy Joel

TURN-OFFS:
People who are superficial, that's the biggest one. Also people who are cheap.

TURN-ONS:
Sense of humor, outgoing personalities, creative people.

BEST GIFT YOU EVER RECEIVED:
Does it count if I didn't get it yet? My sister is getting me a new camera. It's that or a collage that a friend of mine made me.

THE HUMAN BEING YOU MOST ADMIRE:
Mom. She does it all. She had a full-time job and also brought us up. My dad helped, but my mom did all the work around the house and worked the same amount as he did.

THE HUMAN BEING YOU MOST DESPISE:
This person I know from school. She broke up my friend and her boyfriend. She's self-centered and manipulative and will do anything to get what she wants. I can't tell you her name.

YOUR GREATEST FEAR:
Losing family or friends. They're the most important things in my life and without them I'd be alone.

FAVORITE RECREATION:
Photography, drawing, dancing, modeling. It's all self-expression. I like to look for a unique perspective, new ways of looking at things.

YOUR LEAST FAVORITE PART OF YOUR BODY:
My feet. Wait, maybe I do like my feet.

BIGGEST PROBLEM FACING YOU TODAY:
Getting a life after school. I know what I want to do, but once I graduate, I don't know how to do it. I have an end but not the means to it.

HOW YOU FEEL ABOUT YOUR PARENTS:
Things are pretty good. We traveled a lot when I was young, so I think that made us close.

THE BEATLE YOU IDENTIFY WITH MOST:
Paul. Because he wants to hold my hand.

HAVE YOU EVER STOLEN ANYTHING:
I stole some of my sister's wardrobe when I went to school. She's a fashion plate.

YOUR MOTTO:
"No regrets." Make the most out of each day.

MEET THE CAR

Neon. CHRYSLER CORPORATION

THE CAR: **Neon**

VEHICLE TYPE: Front-engine, front-wheel drive, four-door sedan

ENGINE TYPE: Single overhead cam, 2.0-liter, fuel-injected, in-line 4-cylinder generating 133 bhp at 6000 rpm.

FUEL ECONOMY: City—26 mpg; Highway—32 mpg

BASE PRICE: $8,900–$11,000

FEATURES: Cab-forward design with spacious interior and increased visibility; standard dual air bags; available with antilock brakes.

PERFORMANCE: Zero to 60 mph in 8.5 seconds; top speed of 118 mph (governor limited).

ENVIRONMENTAL IMPACT: Elimination of chlorofluorocarbon-producing refrigerants; use of water-based paints; coded plastic parts for improved recycling; minimized use of painted parts for increased recyclability; innovative program of recycling plant packaging, sheet metal scraps, and plastic scraps.

Part 2

Freewheelin'

roadtr!p

DAY 1:

Sunday, September 26:

Boston, MA, to Walden Woods

TRAVEL: 30 miles/25 minutes raw drive time.

Welcome to Road Trip. Fasten your seatbelts and extinguish all smoking materials. Keep all extremities inside the car at all times.

The following is a rough itinerary of your journey. Listed are places to eat, sleep, and hang out along the way. Choose whatever suits your fancy or something completely different. There are only a few rules:

1. While most everything is a suggested stop, you will find an occasional event highlighted by an arrow (→). This indicates a stop that is HIGHLY suggested . . . wink, wink.

2. This list is by no means exhaustive. In fact, it's pretty thin compared to what you'll see on the road, but it will give you a starting point. Feel free to deviate as long as you keep in mind the production schedule.

3. As it is critical to keep all production vehicles together while we're on the road, J.D. has a few words of advice: Think of yourself like an elephant in the circus. Grab the tail of the elephant in front of you and hang on. Beware of pachyderm pies.

Wade, J.D. will give you keys to the Neon
and directions to find your trip-mates. Once
we have completed boarding and reach cruising altitude, feel free to recline your
seat and move about the cabin.

PLACES OF INTEREST:
- **Faneuil Hall**, Boston, an outdoor market with
shops and eats. Congress and South Market streets.
- **Cambridge**, Massachusetts, home of Harvard
University, is just across the Charles River. Innu-
merable bookstores, pubs, and coffee shops.
- **Harvard Square**, Cambridge, is the hub of the university. Plenty of outdoor cafes, overqualified
street musicians, and the occasional eccentric.
- **Crow Haven Corner**, Salem, Massachusetts, is a
grocery store for witches. Laurie Cabat, author of
the book *Power of the Witch*, operates the store.
Stock up on wing of bat. 125 Essex Street.
(508)745-8763.
- **The Christian Science Center** is renowned for
housing one of the finest newspapers in the country
as well as one of America's largest pipe organs. 175
Huntington Street at Massachusetts Avenue.
(617)450-2000.

PLACES TO EAT:
- **Brandy Pete's**. New England fare at reasonable
prices. 267 Franklin Street. (617)439-4165.
- **Durgin Park**. Cafeteria-style eating. 5 Faneuil
Hall Marketplace. (617)227-2038.
- **No Name Restaurant**. Communal tables for
great, cheap Boston seafood. 15½ Fish Pier.
(617)338-7539.

NIGHTLIFE:
- **Wally's Cafe and Jazz Club**, Boston, has a
rotating cast of some of the finest local musicians
and music-school players you'll ever hear. 427
Massachusetts Avenue.
- **Bill's Bar**, a college hangout with a great jukebox. 7 Lansdowne Street. (617)421-9678.
- **Axis**. Dieter says, "You may touch my monkey. Now,
we dance." Wear as much black as possible. 15 Lansdowne Street. (617)262-2437.
- **Dad's Beantown Diner** is an upscale hangout
favored by Celtics and other local celebs. 911 Boyl-
ston Street. (617)296-3237.

→ Leave the city and head for **Walden Woods**, where
you might contemplate the meaning of our accelerated American culture amid the awesome nature that
inspired Henry David Thoreau and Ralph Waldo Emer-
son. Concord, Massachusetts.

ACCOMMODATIONS:
- Camp at **Harold Parker State Forest**. It's just out-
side the city in North Reading, 20 minutes from
Walden Woods.

FADE IN:
EXTERIOR BOSTON—MORNING

The city of Boston is gray and wet. Rain
falls harder than it has in weeks. Eileen
is still packing in her dorm room at Boston
College. Cheri, Brad, and Wade are waking
in dim hotel rooms spread out around the
city.

At 8:30 A.M. Wade receives the keys to the
Neon and directions to Boston College,
where Eileen is waiting for him. After
about an hour and a half of wrong turns and
one-way nightmares along the city's byzan-
tine streets, he pulls up to an old, stone
church where Eileen is waiting beneath her
umbrella.

Wade runs out to help her with her bags.

WADE: You must be Eileen.

EILEEN: Hi. You must be Wade. How's it
going?

WADE: Wet. Let's get going.

INTERIOR NEON—MOMENTS LATER

WADE: What a way to start off.

Today was the longest day of my life! This trip is the most exciting thing that has ever happened to me. I've been on Cloud 9 since I found out that I was chosen! Not only am I getting to travel across America, seeing and doing all kinds of wild things, I'm doing it with three complete strangers AND it's all being filmed. Everyone dreams of being on TV (at least I always have)! And I'm actually getting to film a television show— INCREDIBLE . . .

EILEEN: I know. Murphy's Law. Watch, it'll follow us to Los Angeles.

WADE: You're a student here, right?

EILEEN: Yeah. Not for the next three weeks, though. I'm going to have a lot of catching up to do when I get back.

WADE: Me too.

EILEEN: Where are we going?

WADE: To pick up the other guy, Brad. He's downtown. You know how to get there? I've been driving around lost all morning.

EILEEN: Yeah, just go straight down this road.

WADE: This is the hardest town to drive in I've ever seen.

An hour and a half, several wrong turns, and a grub stop at McDonald's later, they pull up in front of Brad's hotel, where he waits beneath the awning.

Wade and Eileen help Brad with his bags. They shake the rain from themselves as they climb into the car and make formal introductions.

WADE: Listen to those horns. Man, driving through town I've just wanted to go WHAAAAA! How do they do this every day? It would make me want to strangle someone.

BRAD: Whoever designed the streets of Boston must have been dyslexic. What part of Oregon are you from?

WADE: Well, I grew up in Warren until I was in the eighth grade. Then we moved to Portland, which is the big city there. I lived

in L.A. for five years. I was in the Air
Force there.

BRAD: Not too many brothers in Portland.

WADE: No, not too many. A friend of mine
just got married and he moved over to the
southeast section of town. His wife is
black and she was just like, "There's
nobody else around."

BRAD: Your friend's white?

WADE: Yeah.

BRAD: Is that a big deal in Oregon?

WADE: I don't know. I don't think so.

BRAD: It is in Georgia.

WADE: Is it?

BRAD: They'll still lynch you in Georgia.

EILEEN: REALLY?!

BRAD: No. That was a slight exaggeration.
But in a small town like where I'm from . . .
my ex-girlfriend was white.

WADE: What if it's the other way around,
where the guy is white?

BRAD: Then it wouldn't be a big deal. My
girlfriend's parents didn't like it at all,
though. They liked me fine before I was
going out with their daughter, but after
that I was a bad person.

WADE: This happened in Atlanta?

BRAD: Yeah, where I go to school.
Atlanta's only forty-five minutes from my
house, though.

WADE: Really? How long have you been living down there?

BRAD: Six months.

WADE: What's the name of the school?

BRAD: De Kalb College. It's a small school. My first year I went to a private college on a tennis scholarship. I was playing tennis as long as I can remember.

EILEEN: That's cool.

BRAD: Yeah, I played number one there and we made the state finals. We didn't go to the national finals because we had to go as a team . . .

WADE: So you got tired of it?

BRAD: I got real tired of it, so I left.

EILEEN: Do you miss it?

BRAD: No. I hate it. I love the sport, but you know when you do something for so long . . . it becomes a job. I liked it in high school because I didn't have to practice much and I was still better than everyone.

WADE: Do you work?

BRAD: Yeah. I work at a restaurant called Grady's.

EILEEN: Have you ever been to Scalini's?

BRAD: No. What's that?

EILEEN: It's an Italian restaurant. It's not a chain. There's only one. I'm not even sure where it is.

WADE: Is it near him?

EILEEN: It's in Georgia.

BRAD: I love Italian food. I love all Italian stuff. I like those *Godfather* movies, all three of them. I can sit at home with my friends and cop the attitude.

WADE: That's what these people up here

remind me of. Hey, there must be a ball game
going on. They've got the lights on.

BRAD: I have a feeling they're gonna get
rained out. So, Irene, what are you majoring in?

EILEEN: It's Eileen. And I'm majoring
in marketing. I want to go into advertising.

BRAD: I'm sorry. I'm bad with names. How
about you, Wade? Where do you work?

WADE: I'm a personal trainer. I'm putting
myself through fire school.

BRAD: You're going to be a fireman?

WADE: Yeah, I'm studying at the Fire Science Academy in Portland. Is anybody hungry?

BRAD: We could stop and get something to
eat.

EILEEN: We should really pick up Cheri
first.

WADE: We could find a drive-thru.

EILEEN: Oh, no. Last time you did that we
were driving around forever.

WADE: We found one, didn't we? I was so
hungry this morning after I picked Eileen
up, I had to get something to eat, so we
drove through a McDonald's.

EILEEN: Yeah, Wade's like, "I need a snack
before lunch." So I figure a snack, something to tide him over. What does he get?
Big Mac. And that's not all, folks. Filet-
O-Fish, a drink . . .

WADE: I get hungry.

BRAD: So what kind of music do you like?

WADE: I like everything. I like rap, alternative, everything.

EILEEN: I like a lot of stuff. How about you?

BRAD: I like everything. I like some rap.

WADE: Dr. Dre?

BRAD: Sometimes. I have to be in the mood for the more hard-core stuff. I also like rock, though.

WADE: Pearl Jam, Nirvana, Stone Temple Pilots, Alice in Chains . . .

BRAD: I like harder stuff like that sometimes, too. I like Nine Inch Nails. I like country music also, though. Some of that harder alternative stuff like Nine Inch Nails or Alice in Chains . . . it's like rap—I have to be in the mood for it. I like U2, though. When it comes to bands, I think U2 is great.

EILEEN: Have you seen them in concert?

BRAD: Yeah, I went to see the Zoo TV tour. That was the most awesome concert I've ever seen. Blew me away.

EILEEN: I didn't like *Zooropa*.

WADE: Yeah, they kind of went out on a limb and *Achtung Baby* was great, but the new one doesn't really make it.

EILEEN: Where is Cheri from?

WADE: Who knows.

BRAD: I'm not supposed to know, but she's from St. Louis.

With relative ease, the guys find Cheri's hotel and load her into the car.

WADE: Here we go, driving around.

CHERI: Where are we going?

EILEEN: Just checking out the city.

BRAD: We're supposed to get to know each other, so let's talk.

WADE: Cheri, we all know each other now, so it's your turn for the inquisition.

CHERI: All right. What do you want to know?

BRAD: What kind of music do you like?

CHERI: A strange variety. I like a lot of old stuff, like Blondie . . .

EILEEN: I like Blondie.

CHERI: I like some new stuff. I like Pearl Jam. I went to Lollapalooza in North Carolina. Was that anywhere near you, Brad?

BRAD: Yeah, that was pretty close to my house. I'm actually closer to North Carolina, South Carolina, and Tennessee than I am to most of Georgia.

WADE: So you're from St. Louis. What do you do there?

CHERI: Right now I'm waitressing at a country bar and I don't even like country music.

BRAD: Uh-oh.

CHERI: I like some of it, like Garth Brooks. I just don't like the whiney kind. Dolly Parton—I can't deal with that.

BRAD: No, I can't deal with Dolly, either. I don't really like women country singers at all. I don't like women rappers. Don't get me wrong; I'm not a male chauvinist or anything. I just don't like it.

The combination of the caffeine from nine cups of coffee, the anticipation which had been building for days, and my antsyness from being ready early had me bouncing off the walls. I stripped down to my underwear and decided to work out. What a sight! Me doing aerobics on the bed in my underwear with headphones on and singing at the top of my lungs.

All the time, crazy thoughts of what these people might be like kept running through my head. Would the girl be a religious fanatic? Would one of the guys be gay? Maybe a hard-core alternative rocker? I knew that it would be a very diverse group of personalities.

EILEEN: Ahhhhhh . . .

BRAD: Seriously. I like Madonna and Whitney Houston and Janet Jackson just fine. I just don't like women rappers.

CHERI: I also work at a tiny little bar in the historic district where they have blues music.

BRAD: I go to school and I wait tables also, but it's not a country bar.

CHERI: Where do you go to school?

BRAD: De Kalb College in Atlanta.

CHERI: Never heard of it. Is it small?

BRAD: It's about the size of Boston University.

WADE: It's that big?

BRAD: Yeah, but it's all spread out. Our colleges are pretty big but they're spread out over . . . like ten square miles.

CHERI: How big is your town?

BRAD: Ever watch "Mayberry, R.F.D."? No, it's small, though. We have all the fast-food restaurants, but we don't have a movie theater in the whole county. And we don't have a mall.

CHERI: You don't have a mall?

BRAD: Well, we have shopping centers.

CHERI: So you do your shopping in the city?

BRAD: I moved to Atlanta six months ago to be closer to my school.

EILEEN: I love your accent, Brad.

BRAD: Girls always love my accent. Y'all are gonna learn a lot about the South on

Earlier, J.D., one of the producers, told me that Wade was the other guy's name (I already knew Brad's), and that he was very muscular, and that I would probably think he was hot. Well, I don't usually trust a guy's opinion of what is "hot." Very muscular—I envisioned a musclehead whose limbs were so bulky that he had to walk with his legs bowed. Not exactly appealing. I figured that J.D. had no clue about my tastes in men. I was pleasantly surprised. When the Neon arrived, three very normal people piled out of the car to greet me. I had been waiting for this moment for weeks and I didn't know what to say . . . how to react . . . and the cameras were rolling. J.D. was right. Wade was hot!

this trip. Southern cooking, we like to wear bow-ties . . . all that.

CHERI: So, Wade, give me your scoop.

WADE: I'm from Portland, Oregon. I'm a personal trainer there and I'm going into the fire department, so I go to the Fire Science Academy there.

EILEEN: I go to Boston College, but I'm from Jersey.

CHERI: You don't sound like you're from there.

EILEEN: I know. I just never picked up the accent. Hey, how are you doing with the navigating up there?

BRAD: Where are we going? Faneuil Hall, right?

WADE: I'm going to pull over and ask.

BRAD: Monday night we have to watch the football game. Atlanta's playing. I'm going out with one of their cheerleaders. Her name's Chrissy.

WADE: Going out with, you mean dating?

BRAD: Well, we're not married or anything. She's just one of the girls I'm dating.

WADE: What do you consider dating?

BRAD: It's just going out and stuff.

WADE: Well is that just a friend, or? . . .

BRAD: It's a friend, but . . . when I say dating I mean a friend that I kiss.

CHERI: When does someone become more than a friend? When it's more than a kiss?

BRAD: No. Sex has nothing to do with the relationship. The relationship is when you

For several hours we tried to get to know each other. I, of course, quickly cleared the air on the sexuality question. Unlike "Real World," none of them are homosexual. (Not that it would matter—I was just trying to figure out what types of people they had chosen.)

are committed to each other. That's the
emotional level of it . . .

CHERI: So we're going to assume that
there's not too high of an emotional level
at this point?

BRAD: There's no emotional level here.

CHERI: I'll stop, because you're going to
get yourself in trouble. So, Eileen, do you
have any "friends"?

EILEEN: Oh, "friends"? Yeah, I'm sort of
seeing someone, but he doesn't go to my
school.

WADE: Where does he go?

EILEEN: He goes to a SUNY school.

WADE: A what?

EILEEN: State University of New York. They
have them all over the place. What about
you?

CHERI: I've been dating someone for three
years.

WADE: You are now?

CHERI: Well, we decided to see other people about four months ago and it hasn't
been going so good since then.

WADE: Why did you do that?

CHERI: I'm too young.

WADE: How old are you?

CHERI: Twenty-four. I just wasn't ready to
settle down.

WADE: Was he ready for marriage?

CHERI: Oh, yeah. Marriage and kids. He's
twenty-eight. But in answer to your question, I would say I don't have a boyfriend.

I have a "friend," as Brad would say. Okay, Wade, your turn.

WADE: Yeah. "Friends." I don't have a girlfriend. I have "friends." Relationships are funny.

CHERI: Yeah, they're gonna be real funny when we get home. My "friend" isn't too happy about me coming on the trip.

WADE: Because you're going to be gone?

CHERI: No, I don't think that's what the big problem is. The big problem is the fact that it's not all girls in the car.

BRAD: He's insecure.

WADE: Did he try to talk you out of it?

CHERI: No, but I was so excited I was bouncing off the walls. I think he felt like I was rubbing it in. Are any of us gay?

WADE: No.

BRAD: Do we look gay?

CHERI: Everyone in St. Louis told me they were going to stick a gay guy in here.

BRAD: Why should you care if we were gay? I don't care if one of y'all is a lesbian.

CHERI: I wouldn't care, but everyone kept saying that, so I thought we'd clear the air now. I thought maybe that was the reason you only have "friends."

The Robert Gould Shaw and 54th Regiment Memorial on Boston Common commemorates the first black combat regiment of the Civil War. The story of the 54th was recounted in the film *Glory*.
COURTESY OF MASSACHUSETTS OFFICE OF TRAVEL AND TOURISM

Our campers finally find their way to Faneuil Hall and sit down at a cafe for dinner.

Wade is eating a salad while the rest wait for their food.

BRAD: Everybody's looking over here because Wade started eating without us.

Seriously, man, it's terribly impolite to eat before we get our food.

WADE: But when you get a salad you have to. It comes first.

BRAD: Yeah, but on a date, the tip is, if I get a meal with a salad, I'll ask for the salad to come with the meal because it's not polite to eat before the lady.

CHERI: Take it from Brad, who's a lady-killer.

BRAD: But you're from Oregon, so we'll let it slide this time. How far is New York from here?

WADE: I think it's like five hours.

The waitress brings along the rest of the food, barely escaping with her fingers as the gang digs in.

BRAD: Y'all gonna wait to say grace?

EILEEN: I said it in my head.

WADE: We'll wait and you can say it aloud next time.

BRAD: I didn't want to say anything . . . I don't know if y'all are atheists or devil worshipers or what.

CHERI: What are you guys . . . any religion?

EILEEN: Catholic.

CHERI: Me too.

BRAD: Southern Baptist.

CHERI: How about you, Wade?

WADE: I'm nothing, really. Nothing formal.

When Eileen and I were waiting to meet up with the guys after shopping, Kurt (the director) wanted to tape us talking about our first impressions of the guys. So, a crowd of about twenty-five people gathered to hear our intimate conversation. Although flattered by the attention, our "girl talk" was somewhat hampered.

BRAD: I don't want to talk about religion. I'll be right.

EILEEN: You're always right, Brad. You eat your fries with a fork?

BRAD: What do you use?

WADE: Fingers. You always do that?

BRAD: Except for like, McDonald's, where they don't give you a fork.

CHERI: In Europe they do. They give you little tiny forks.

WADE: You've been to Europe?

CHERI: Yeah. I backpacked through there.

EILEEN: What part?

CHERI: Germany, Italy, Switzerland, France.

WADE: How long?

CHERI: A month.

WADE: By yourself?

CHERI: My best friend went with me.

WADE: When did you go?

CHERI: Right after high school—'87. It was cool. We traveled all over. We had a Eurail pass and we would sleep on the train sometimes or camp out or sometimes get a hotel.

WADE: I should have gotten french fries. Is that pizza good?

EILEEN: It's really good. Want some?

WADE: I'm just waiting.

CHERI: I'll take a bite of yours, Wade.

Due to rain, we couldn't camp out, so we stayed in a hotel on the outskirts of Boston. The four of us were set free—no cameras on us—so we went to the hotel bar and had drinks, which led to the guys' room when the bar closed. We talked till late and climbed from room to room across the balconies.

WADE: Um . . . okay.

CHERI: Just a little one.

Cheri takes a "little" bite of Wade's sandwich. He stares after it longingly.

FADE OUT.

DAY 2:

Monday, September 27:

Boston, MA, to New York

TRAVEL: 220 miles/4.4 hours raw drive time

PLACES OF INTEREST:
- **Mystic Seaport**, Connecticut, an old fishing village, aquarium, and home of Mystic Pizza. It's also
home to the U.S. Naval base where most of America's
nuclear subs were manufactured.
- **Old Sturbridge Village**, Sturbridge, Massachusetts, a Colonial town where men wear triangular
hats and the women wear bonnets. They reenact life
in the 1830s.
- **The Motorcycle Museum** highlights the Indian
Motorcycle Company's contribution to two-wheeled
fun. 33 Hendee Street. Springfield, Massachusetts.
(413)737-2624.
- **The Nut Museum** at 303 Ferry Road in Old Lyme, Connecticut, is home to Elizabeth Tashjian. You've
seen her on Letterman and Carson as The Nut Lady.
You can visit her house/museum and meet her in person. (203)434-7636; call in advance.

→ **FARM HANDS–CITY HANDS/GREEN CHIMNEYS** is an
organic farm dedicated to linking farm and city for
the social, cultural, economic, and environmental
enrichment of people from different socio-economic
backgrounds. Have lunch with the kids who run the
farm. Brewster, New York.

PLACES TO EAT:
New York:
- **Two Boots Cafe**, Italian food, located in the Lower
East Side. 37 Avenue A. (212)505-2276.
- **Caribe**, Jamaican food, located between Perry
Street and Greenwich Avenue. (212)255-9191.
- **Caliente Cab Company**, Mexican, on Bleecker and
6th Avenue. (212)243-8517.

Cheri, Brad, and Wade mug for the camera
with kids from Farm Hands—City Hands.

- **Mi Cocina**, Mexican, Jane Street and 9th Avenue. (212)627-8273.
- **The Lucky Strike** in SoHo is a late-night hangout, open till 4:00 A.M. Grand Street between Wooster Street and West Broadway. (212)941-0742.
- **The Rainbow Room** in the NBC building has a commanding view of the Empire State Building. (You'll recognize it from *Sleepless in Seattle*.) (212)632-5100.
- For ethnic treats, there are countless bistros and restaurants in **Little Italy** and **Chinatown**.

NIGHTLIFE:
- **Cafe Wha**, an early haunt of Bob Dylan's, is still a cool bar with live music. Minetta Lane and MacDougal Street. (212)254-3630.
- **Wetlands** is the place to see the Spin Doctors and their psychedelic ilk. Located in TriBeCa, it features eco-drinking, with an environmental information center in an old VW bus that sits in the bar. 161 Hudson Street. (212)966-4225.
- **The Limelight** was once a gothic cathedral. Now it's a den of iniquity, with drinks, dancing, and girls gyrating in cages hung from the ceiling. They kept the stained glass. 20th Street and 6th Avenue. (212)807-7850.
- Looking for adventure? Try **Downtown Beirut** at 158 First Avenue in the East Village. It's the best jukebox in the city. 10th Street and 1st Avenue. (212)260-4248.
- **McSorley's** is the city's oldest bar. They never clean it. They have dust from the 1800s and cheap, strong ale. (212)473-9148.

ACCOMMODATIONS:
- **The Chelsea Hotel** has a long, artistic history. Mark Twain, Arthur Miller, Thomas Wolfe, Tennessee Williams, Jimi Hendrix, The Grateful Dead, and Jackson Pollock have all stayed here. While in residence, Arthur C. Clarke wrote the screenplay for *2001: A Space Odyssey*. William S. Burroughs wrote *Naked Lunch* here. Of more recent fame, Sid Vicious offed his girlfriend here. 222 West 23rd Street. (212)243-3700.
- **The Carlton Arms** at 160 East 25th Street is a clean, bargain hotel with an arty clientele who have painted the whole place with murals. (212)697-0680.
- **Chelsea Center Youth Hostel** is a small, safe hostel on the Lower West Side.

FADE IN:
INTERIOR NEON—MORNING

Having spent the night getting to know each
other, our travelers set out on a wet morning for New York City.

CHERI: I didn't realize Portland was a
fairly small town.

WADE: Yeah, whenever they do those lists
of the top ten cities to live, or top twenty
cities . . . it's always on it.

CHERI: St. Louis was one of the top ten
places for singles on one of those lists.

WADE: Really?

CHERI: And if that's true, it's a sad
state of affairs. I was thinking of joining
this thing called the St. Louis Athletic
Social Club. My friend is in it. They go to
hockey games and football games, have fund-
raisers with touch football, things like
that.

Wade and Brad load up the car for the ride
out of Boston. EILEEN CHUNG

WADE: Like through a gym? It's a meat market—but not in a bar?

CHERI: No, not through the gym. It's just
a bunch of young professionals. It's a way
of networking. Then again, right now I
don't feel like a young professional,
either. Maybe I'll wait. I'm not looking forward to joining the dating scene
again.

WADE: I went out on a blind date not long
ago and when I got there, I was like,
"Ughhh." We went out to this dance club . . .

BRAD: Was she ugly?

WADE: Oh, yeah. And she had real big hair,
you know, with the bangs coming out at you?

My First Impressions:

EILEEN—20 (somewhat young). Very quiet, seems pristine, conservative, easy to get along with, very modest (won't change her clothes in front of me). I'm relieved that she seems like someone I can get along with. BRAD—21 (even younger). Very argumentative, athletic, tries to impress (especially Eileen—he seems to have the hots for her), mentally typical of good-looking guy his age. WADE—27 (seems mature). Gorgeous, great body, somewhat reserved (definite attraction). We flirted a lot.

EILEEN: Oh, that's the worst. That's a total New Jersey look.

WADE: So we're just sitting at this table and she just leans over and starts to kiss me. What am I going to do? I pulled away and I'm like, "We're in a bar and I hardly know you." She sits back like she's offended. Then, after a while she goes, "You want to dance?" So we go dance and she does that thing where they turn away from you and put their hands on their knees . . .

BRAD: Yeah!

WADE: I just turned around like I wasn't even dancing with her. She was scary.

CHERI: Blind date from hell?

WADE: I told her I had a softball tournament the next day and I had to be home by ten-thirty.

EILEEN: How did you end up with her?

WADE: She was a friend of this girl that my friend was chasing. Guys will do that to you all the time. They want the good-looking one and they'll tell you anything. They'll be like, "She's not so bad, man, come on, do me a favor."

BRAD: I got stuck like that once. Man, she was ugly. She was this skinny little girl with red hair, freckles, pale as this piece of paper. When she showed up at my door, my roommate just started laughing.

EILEEN: Okay. I don't think we need to hear more about that.

BRAD: She didn't know what he was laughing at.

EILEEN: That's beside the point. That's mean.

BRAD: It's not mean if she don't know. But, man, she was something.

WADE: The worst is when you think they're good-looking and then you find out something about them that just totally turns you off.

BRAD: Yeah I know exactly. I know this one girl I thought was real good-looking until we saw her in a bikini and she had zits all over her back.

EILEEN: That's so unfair. Guys have things like that. Like a guy with so much hair on his chest it looks like a rug . . .

BRAD: I ain't got but five hairs on my chest and it took me twenty-one years to grow 'em.

WADE: Now a girl with hair on her chest, that would be something.

BRAD: You went out with a girl like that?

WADE: No! If I did, I would've taken a picture of it.

EILEEN: You're so bad.

BRAD: You just know you like me *(singing)* Eileen's gone black boy crazy, I've gone Chinese girl hazy. We've got Jungle Fever . . .

EILEEN: I never saw that whole movie. I missed the ending.

WADE: I like Spike Lee.

BRAD: That was one of the dumbest movies I ever saw. That had nothing to do with interracial relationships. Spike Lee is prejudiced as hell. And the whole thing was that the relationship didn't work because

We had to get out of the camera car and get into the "exterior" car. It doesn't have cameras or tinted windows. We drove a block away and waited for the "go ahead" from the walkie-talkie. Then we arrived for a second time, so that they could film us arriving. I have a feeling this doing things over in the exterior car is going to become a daily routine.

Wesley Snipes was cheating on his wife. Didn't have anything to do with her color. The story was he cheats on his wife with his secretary, who happens to be Italian. She wants him to move out on his wife, which he does for a while, but then he goes back to his wife. End of movie. That has nothing to do with race. People do it all the time.

EILEEN: But it's the reasons why he cheated. He wasn't just cheating, it was because she was white.

BRAD: Believe me, there's only one reason you cheat and it doesn't have so much to do with color. I'm an only child, so I was always kind of spoiled. Then, two years ago, my dad found out he had an illegitimate daughter, so we got sued in a big way.

WADE: No way! How'd he find that out?

BRAD: Papers came in the mail suing him for back child support. It was so messed up. Georgia laws are messed up.

CHERI: So you have a half-sister?

BRAD: I don't claim her. If you ask my dad how many kids he has, he'll say, "One."

CHERI: How old is she?

BRAD: She should be about fourteen by now. That rocked my world, man. When we got sued, my mom went from driving a Mercedes to not driving a car at all.

WADE: Wait. If she's only fourteen . . .

BRAD: Yeah, my parents went through problems with that. They worked through it, though.

EILEEN: Have you ever met her?

> Again, eating was stressful—the cameras just sit there, focused on you. Sometimes you feel that you have nothing interesting to say and then other times you just worry about whether you have food stuck in your teeth or not. I can see it now: me just yapping away on national TV with a big piece of pepper stuck between my front teeth.

BRAD: No. Don't care to, either. I hated her for a long time.

The Neon turns into the driveway of Farm Hands—City Hands/Green Chimneys in Brewster, NY.

CUT TO:

INTERIOR NEON—EVENING

Leaving Brewster behind, Brad points the car south, toward New York City.

BRAD: Y'all better not fall asleep on me. I'm gonna start singing. I'm warning you.

EILEEN: Okay, tell me about your childhood.

BRAD: What do you want to know?

EILEEN: I don't know. Anything.

BRAD: Well, I had a happy childhood; pretty much kept myself amused. Both of my parents were pretty much there for me. I had what you would call a "normal" childhood. I was into sports. I played baseball, tennis, football, basketball. I played all that up through high school, then I just played tennis and basketball. I dropped the rest.

EILEEN: Who's your favorite player?

BRAD: In basketball? Magic Johnson or Larry Bird. They don't play anymore, but they're my all-time favorite players.

EILEEN: Shaq?

BRAD: I haven't seen Shaquille play enough. I'm not one to follow along with the crowd.

EILEEN: That Pepsi commercial is really cool.

BRAD: Yeah. I have to get to know them, though. I look at the way a player acts outside the court and all that. That's why I like Magic and Larry Bird. They're class acts. Who's your favorite?

EILEEN: I don't know if I have one. My sister's is Scottie Pippen.

BRAD: He's got a head like Frankenstein.

EILEEN: That's not nice.

BRAD: It's true, though. You ever see that block head he's got? What about your favorite actor?

EILEEN: Richard Gere . . . Tom Cruise. How about you?

BRAD: I've got a whole list. I don't think I could pick just one. I like a lot of old actors. I like Gregory Peck, Henry Fonda, John Wayne, James Cagney, Humphrey Bogart, Spencer Tracy, Errol Flynn . . . I like old movies better than new ones. As far as newer actors, I like Tom Cruise. At first I didn't. After *Top Gun*, all of his movies were kind of the same.

EILEEN: I didn't like *Cocktail*. Actually he's supposed to be in that new vampire movie. I heard the writer, Anne Rice, didn't think he was right for it.

BRAD: I like Denzel Washington. I think he's one of the best actors of our time. I like Larry Fishburn, Wesley Snipes, Morgan Freeman . . . do you know who he is?

EILEEN: No.

BRAD: He was in *Driving Miss Daisy* and he

J.D. told us that we were staying in a totally cool hotel with eccentric art on the walls, THE CARLTON ARMS. I had envisioned a fancy hotel (like the Ritz) with expensive art on the walls, not a hole-in-the-wall in downtown N.Y. with murals drawn all over.

was in that Clint Eastwood movie *Unfor-given*. Danny Glover . . .

EILEEN: I don't know who he is, either.

BRAD: He was in the *Lethal Weapon* movies.

EILEEN: I didn't see them.

BRAD: Sidney Poitier. Al Pacino . . . little guy with a big attitude.

EILEEN: He was great in *Scarface*.

Silence prevailed for the next few minutes as the crew stared out the window at the landscape.

BRAD: Wait till we get to Georgia and meet my folks. I still have this perception of my dad . . . you always have these perceptions of your parents from the time that you were a little kid. He was always a good man, but he was strict, strait-laced, no gray, just black and white, wrong and right, and that's the way he was with me when I was growing up. But now, he's not as mean. He's just tempered. Working in the prison, he had a reputation as a mean man. Now, he can't even bring himself to kill a deer anymore. That's how soft he's getting. He's a trip.

WADE: How old is he?

BRAD: Forty-nine. And he's country, too, like you've never seen. He's country, happy, smiling all the time. He's cool.

FADE OUT.

Brad, Cheri, and Wade hold conference in the shower stall of the Carlton Arms Hotel. EILEEN CHUNG

Wade's a good dancer (actually moves well). In my platforms, I'm about his size—we looked good together—people stared. Saw Sean Penn's brother, then left at 4:30 A.M. Couldn't believe we got the same cabbie that had dropped us off two hours earlier. Secretly smooched. Not getting much sleep tonight.

DAY 3:

TRAVEL: 235 miles/4.7 hours raw drive time

PLACES OF INTEREST:
New York:
- **Central Park** before dark is a great place for rollerblading, biking, and people watching.
- While in Central Park, check out **Strawberry Fields**, at the 72nd Street entrance. This patch of the park is a tribute to John Lennon, who lived across the street at the Dakota.
- **Greenwich Village** is a hub of culture in the Big Apple. Start at the intersection of Bleecker and MacDougal streets.
- **St. Mark's Place** is the strip of offbeat shops and street vendors for some pre-road shopping. 8th Street between 2nd and 3rd avenues.
- **The Statue of Liberty** is accessible through the Circle Line at Battery Park.
- **The Metropolitan Museum of Art**, one of the world's finest museums, is located adjacent to Central Park at 81st Street.
- **The Guggenheim Museum** is known primarily for its architecture, a Frank Lloyd Wright design that stands out even in New York. Most of the permanent collection is Impressionist and later. 5th Avenue and 88th Street.
- The **Lower East Side Tenement Museum** is the place to delve into the city's immigrant past, and present. At 97 Orchard Street.
- **The New York Public Library** and the ever-vigilant lions at the entrance sit at the corner of 5th Avenue and 42nd Street.

Sometimes I wish I wasn't so attracted to Wade. I find that I'm not being myself. It's just one more pressure to deal with. Also, I am careful about what I say when the cameras are on. I have to be realistic—everyone will see this— parents, grandma, and many who don't know me that well. Refraining from talking about things I don't want to be public knowledge.

On the road:
- Baltimore's Inner Harbor is the home of the **National Aquarium**, one of the largest attractions in the United States.
- Philadelphia, Pennsylvania, is home to the **National Shrine of Saint John Neumann**, where a wax replica of His Holiness encases his skeleton.

PLACES TO EAT:
New York:
- No trip to New York is complete without lunch or breakfast at a Jewish deli. **Katz's Deli** on Houston Street defines the genre.

On the road:
- More than just a hamburger joint, White Castle Hamburgers on Route 1 in Edison, New Jersey, is a cultural institution.
- **Cluck-U-Chicken**: The name says it all. Franklin Park, New Jersey. (908)297-8111.
- **Pat's King of Steaks**, The Original—9th and Wharton streets in Philadelphia—is the place to grab a foot-long roll filled with thin-cut steak, onions, and Velveeta. Yum. (215)468-1546.

Washington, DC:
- **Maison Blanche**, Nice and French. 1725 F Street. (202)842-0700.
- **Caribe**, Caribbean food. 2004 18th Street. (202)387-1130.
- **Perry's**, Sushi with rooftop dining in Adams Morgan. 1811 Columbia Road. (202)234-6218.
- **The Childe Harold**, hangout long renowned for attracting radicals with British flair. DuPont Circle, 1610 20th Street. (202)483-6700.

NIGHTLIFE:
Washington:
- **The Brickskeller** has five hundred different brands of beer from around the world, as well as good, simple bar food. (202)293-1885.
- **930 Night Club**, 930 F Street NW, has a big rep as the alternative venue. (202)638-2008.
- **The Tune Inn** is a divy, funky hangout for up-and-coming pages, congressional aides, and others aspiring to the Hill, 33½ Pennsylvania Avenue SE. (202)543-2725.
- **Irish Times** is a great Irish pub. 14 F Street. (202)543-5433.
- **Millie and Al's**, good, raunchy, blue-

> Brad and I are getting along better. At first we kind of clashed, but things seem like they're smoothing out. Brad has the hots for Eileen, but she isn't interested.

collar bar, in Adams Morgan. 2440 18th Street NW.
(202)387-8131.
- **Third Edition**, a singles meat market in Georgetown at 1218 Wisconsin Avenue. (202)333-3700.
- **The Tombs** is a Georgetown student hangout. 1226
36th Street. (202)337-6668.

ACCOMMODATIONS:
- **Washington International AYH Youth Hostel** is
clean and very central. At 1426 H Street NW.
(202)783-6016.
- **Motel 6**, 75 Hampton Park Boulevard, Capitol
Heights, Maryland. (301)499-0800.

FADE IN:
INTERIOR NEON—AFTERNOON

After spending the day sightseeing in New
York, the road trippers start on the five-
hour journey to the nation's capital.

Somewhere on the New Jersey Turnpike, Wade
deals with the age-old question: Why didn't
you go before we left?

Wade climbs back into the car after leaving
to relieve himself on the side of the road.

CHERI: You're in bare feet now?

WADE: I had to. I accidentally peed on my
socks.

The rest of the car laughs.

WADE: There was a branch in my way.

CHERI: You peed on your socks? I thought
you were joking.

WADE: No, there was a branch in the way
and I didn't see it. So when I started to
go . . .

> I am ready to get on the road—totally in a bad mood. My feet hurt, my hose were run, I'm tired and look like hell. I'm not the prissy type, but I'm finding myself constantly primping—I want to look good on TV.

CHERI: (laughing) That's too funny.

They pull back onto the highway.

Wade, sitting behind Cheri, stretches his feet into the front seat.

CHERI: Are these clean?

WADE: Yeah. Except I haven't showered in two days. And I've been walking around on them all day.

CUT TO:

INTERIOR NEON—NIGHT

Having filled themselves up at Burger King and gassed up the car, the crew plugs on toward Washington.

EILEEN: So Wade, have you thought about marriage at all?

WADE: (*laughing*) No . . . yeah, thought about it . . .

EILEEN: Just thought about it?

WADE: I always thought I'd be married by this point. Just hasn't turned out that way, I guess.

EILEEN: Yeah. I'm thinking around twenty-eight, but . . .

WADE: Yeah, that's the thing, you just don't know.

EILEEN: You don't know. If the person's not there, you can't just look at your watch and say, "I'm twenty-eight!"

WADE: I used to think by the time I was twenty-six or twenty-seven, I'd be married and have kids.

Male-bonding in the Big Apple. EILEEN CHUNG

EILEEN: How many kids do you want?

WADE: Three.

EILEEN: All boys?

WADE: Mixed. As long as I have one to carry on the name, that's all right.

EILEEN: Wade junior?

WADE: I like kids. It's not that I'm afraid of marriage, I just haven't found the right person. I'm hoping by the time I'm thirty, anyway.

EILEEN: That's barely time to plan a wedding.

WADE: That's a woman's wedding. I mean, you don't have to take two years to plan everything out.

EILEEN: You have to reserve a church and everything . . .

Brad, groggy, chimes in.

BRAD: That's a Catholic wedding. Normal folks' weddings don't take two years to plan. That's just Catholic. The Pope told 'em that.

WADE: Besides that, weddings . . . they make such a big deal out of it.

EILEEN: They're like proms.

WADE: And you blow all this cash for what? So you can stand up in front of everybody and say, "I *dooo?*"

WADE: Would you marry someone who isn't Chinese?

EILEEN: Yeah.

WADE: Is your boyfriend Chinese?

EILEEN: Yeah. He's my first Chinese boyfriend, though. I just met him this summer. It's weird, because around me there aren't that many Asians at all, so I just grew up like that. I mean, there were a few, but nobody I was really attracted to. And I'm his first Asian girlfriend, too.

BRAD: The majority of my girlfriends have always been white. I date black girls, too, but I never started getting serious with a white girl until that first girl, Lauren.

EILEEN: Is that the cheerleader?

BRAD: No. See, except for Lauren I never got serious about a white girl. I'd just mess around with them, but all my serious girlfriends were black. Those were the girls that I took home and took to the prom and everything. But behind closed doors I was messing with white girls.

WADE: When I was living in Arizona I knew this white girl who only dated black guys. And then, one day—out of the blue—she marries this white guy. I was like, "Whoa."

BRAD: It's wild. I'm not gonna sit here and say who I'm gonna marry. Me and my friends were talking about this. I would marry who I fell in love with. No matter what color she was . . . black, white, Asian or Hispanic. If I fell in love with her, I would marry her.

WADE: What if you brought her home and your mom and dad said, "*Nooo* way?"

BRAD: Well, that's what happened when I brought Lauren home.

The Statue of Liberty holds her torch above Liberty Island in New York Harbor. EILEEN CHUNG

WADE: Really?

BRAD: See, my dad always knew that I had black girls that were my girlfriends and that I was sneaking around with white girls on the side. And he was always like, "That's my boy!" But I had never gotten serious with a white girl and brought her home and said, "This is my girlfriend." And when I did that, he was . . . he was quiet. My mom hit the roof.

WADE: She did?

BRAD: Oh, yeah. My mom hit the roof, all my aunts hit the roof, my girl cousins . . . my guy cousins didn't care, but my girl cousins . . . they went ape.

WADE: Your parents probably thought that . . . you're young, she's young . . . you'll grow out of it. If you came in and said you were going to marry her? The hammer would have come down.

BRAD: My dad was cool. He just said, "Look, I raised you to have your own values. I ain't even gonna tell you my opinion because it don't count." My mom, though, she was like, "I'm gonna give you my opinion. I don't like her, I don't trust her . . . "

WADE: That's probably what her dad said about you, too.

BRAD: That's what her mom AND dad said about me. Her mom was straight-up and said, "I don't like you dating because he's black." Her dad was a teacher at the high school and he went the other route. He said, "I don't want you dating him because him and his friends have a reputation for screwing around with girls and dumping them."

EILEEN: Is that true, Brad?

BRAD: (*ignoring her*) He thought I was just gonna use her and carve another notch in my bedpost. Then, though, when it didn't happen like that and we stayed together, he gave his real feelings on the subject.

EILEEN: What were you saying about high school?

Brad begins to whistle nonchalantly.

EILEEN: Dodging the subject!

BRAD: I don't care. I was a dog in high school. I was a D-O-G. I was a scrawny, skinny little dog . . . walking around, talking junk . . . I'm surprised someone didn't beat the living hell out of me in high school.

WADE: Bow-wow-wow.

BRAD: To get back, though, I think it's more accepted for a white guy to date a black girl than vice versa. I have this friend, Brett. He's white. We're good friends. I mean, his parents call me son. Now Brett used to date this black girl and that was all right. But if his sister, Robin, ever brought home a black guy, his father would shoot him before he came in the door.

EILEEN: No way.

BRAD: And they love me, but I've never messed with her. I guarantee if they ever even heard that me and her were messing around, they would turn on me just like that. And they've known me all my life.

My turn to drive—rush hour in N.Y.—I about died. I would be cruising along and all of a sudden my lane would begin to disappear. Once a bus and a cab tried to edge me out—Wade kept yelling to gas it, but looking at these cabs and buses with tons of dents and dings I realized that they don't care if they hit you.

WADE: That's messed up.

They stop and pay another toll. Brad continues.

BRAD: It's weird, 'cause some of my friends now, you should hear them talk about Mexicans. My friend Casey, I love him to death, but the biggest thing we fuss about is that he's prejudiced as hell against Mexicans. He's all, "Wetback this and spick this, lazy, ten of them live in an apartment . . . " And I'm just like, "What's up with that?" It's just pure ignorance because he doesn't know any Mexicans.

EILEEN: Well, where does he get his attitude from?

BRAD: I don't know. See, he used to be that way about Laotians, too, and he didn't know any of them. But there was this one Laotian guy in our school, Razamee, cool as a fan, man.

EILEEN: (*laughing*) You got the sayings down.

BRAD: Serious. He was cool. He would be chillin' with me and I would introduce him to all my friends and I had a lot of white friends. So he started chillin' with them and they got along and then after Razamee, everyone started accepting Laotians. And these same people used to slur on all the Laotians. But now, it's Mexicans. It's a trip, how it works.

WADE: Yeah, it's screwed.

BRAD: That's my main tick since moving to Atlanta about dating a black girl—'cause I went out with a couple of hot black girls—

but I couldn't get serious with them because they were prejudiced against whites. If you say something against the white race, then you're automatically offending me like you said something against the black race. I get into it with black people all the time.

WADE: See, that offends some people. That stuff wouldn't offend me in the least. If a black guy or an Asian called me a cracker, it would just make me laugh. I wouldn't even take offense to it. I think people put too much emphasis on a name.

BRAD: The thing is, though, it's not so much the name . . .

WADE: It's the intention behind it.

BRAD: Yeah. See, I'm big on respect. I'm REAL big on respect. If you don't respect me, we're gonna have a big problem. I can deal with prejudiced people all day. I know a lot of people who just hate me because I'm black. And that's cool, as long as they don't say anything to me, we're fine. I have a bigger problem with someone trying to be cool or pretending to be down, then getting mad at another black person and saying something about me behind my back. That's racist.

WADE: That's wild. I don't even see it really, where I live. Well, you know where I see it? When I'm the minority. Like if I go down to play basketball at some of the courts in town, it's kind of funny how quick it turns. The minute that there's more blacks than whites, it's amazing how prejudiced they become. They just don't want to play. They don't say any-

thing, you just never touch the ball. It's
obvious.

BRAD: It was weird for me, too, though.
'Cause I was never around all blacks. I was
raised in an all-white environment, just
about. I didn't have that much experience
being around blacks.

WADE: Is there like a lot of conflict
there?

BRAD: See, Habersham County where I grew
up is one of those places where they really
don't have that many racial problems. Once
in a while something will come up, but usually the whites look at it like everybody's
okay as long as they stay in their place.
So, it's like, you've got one black neighborhood, and as long as the blacks stay
there, everything's all right.

WADE: That's a bad attitude.

BRAD: But then, everybody gets along. Like
in high school, as long as the blacks
played football, basketball, and ran
track, they were all right. The white parents loved them as long as they played
those sports . . . and didn't mess with
their daughters. But then they resented me,
because when I got to high school, I
quit playing football and just played tennis . . . and basketball. Then I was number
one in tennis and they hated that. A lot of
parents—white parents—in the community
started not liking me. I didn't "stay in my
place" as they put it. All the other black
guys would come to school saggin' their
jeans, high-top tennis shoes, T-shirts, and
hat down over their eyes. I would come to
school wearing Polo shirts and penny

The 555-foot Washington Monument is probably the most recognizable attraction in the nation's capital. The elevator to the top takes 70 seconds, while the 897-step stairway to the bottom takes considerably longer, especially if you stop to read all 200 memorial plaques. COURTESY OF THE WASHINGTON, DC CONVENTION AND VISITORS ASSOCIATION (1991)

loafers. Then, I went to their parties. So, like, they would have a party for their daughters and I would show up with my boys and I'm not dressed like a gangster . . . they didn't like that at all. They would say, "He thinks he's better than the other blacks," and that started turning the blacks in my own neighborhood against me. 'Cause they would be all, "What's up with that? You think you're better than us? You're too pretty to play football?" And I grew up with them. But they didn't realize that all that stuff, a lot of it, the white teachers were putting it in their heads, to try to get me to say, "All right, I'll sag, I'll play football." I had it coming from both sides.

EILEEN: Hey, I just noticed we're really low on gas.

The car falls silent for a few moments.

WADE: Man, eighty more miles. So much for getting there early.

FADE OUT.

DAY 4:

TRAVEL: 304 miles, 6.1 hours raw drive time

PLACES OF INTEREST:
Washington, DC:
- **The Awakening** is a sculpture of a huge human emerging from the earth, a head here, an arm there, a leg there . . . at Hains Point, East Potomac Park.
- **The Vietnam Veterans Memorial** is more than a tribute—it's an incredible work of art located near the Lincoln Memorial.
- **The Bureau of Printing and Engraving** is the place they crank out all those beautiful bills in your wallet. Millions of dollars every day are printed, cut, inspected, and sent into circulation. 14th and C streets SW. (202)874-3017.
- **Ford's Theater**, where Booth shot Lincoln. 511 10th Street NW. (202)638-2941.
- **Washington Monument** is on the Mall, opposite the Lincoln Memorial.
- **Lincoln Memorial** sits on the Potomac. Maybe you remember Clint's conversation with Abe in *In the Line of Fire.* At the end of the Mall.
- **Potato Museum**. Visit Mister and Missus Potato Head themselves, Tom and Meredith Hughes, as you tour their cellar full of potatoes and potato-related paraphernalia. By appointment only. 704 North Carolina Avenue SE. (202)544-1558.
- **The White House**. Meet Bill, Hillary, and the whole gang. Suggested housewarming gift: McDonald's. 1600 Pennsylvania Avenue.

→ In Adams Morgan, the Greenwich Village of Washington, be on the lookout for **Blelvis**, a street person claiming to be the black reincarnation of The King.

We are ALWAYS lost. It's unbelievable—a caravan of six and we can't get the directions right. Spent an hour driving in circles.

Virginia:
- Just off I-81 is the **Museum at New Market Battlefield**, where the bloody story of the Civil War is told in detail at the site of a legendary confrontation that involved a company of fourteen-year-old cadet/soldiers from the Virginia Military Institute.
- Roanoke is home to the **largest man-made illuminated star**. It stands 88½ feet tall on a mountaintop.
→ Try the scenic **Skyline Drive** along the crest of the Blue Ridge Mountains and look out over Shenandoah National Park.

PLACES TO EAT:
- **The Rowe Family Restaurant**, Staunton, Virginia, on Route 250. (703)886-1833.
- **The Roanoker**, in Roanoke, is a fine country cafe at 2522 Colonial Avenue. (703)344-7746.

ACCOMMODATIONS:
- **Motel 6**, Roanoke, Virginia, just off Peter's Creek Parkway at Fairlane. (703)563-2871.

Kurt told us that they had arranged lunch on Capitol Hill with some congresspeople. Wade said he would go, but not talk. Brad echoed him. I knew Eileen wouldn't say much, so I felt the pressure was on me to make sure we didn't look like clueless idiots. Lunch went OK. No one but me ate on camera. Afterward, J.D. said that the boys wanted to talk to us about something. When I confronted them they wouldn't say anything. It was difficult, because I couldn't say, "J.D. said you had something to tell us." On camera, we can't talk about the crew. It's supposed to be like

---

FADE IN:
INTERIOR CAPITOL BUILDING—DAY

After visiting the Bureau of Printing and Engraving, the cast walks to Capitol Hill for a pizza-and-Coke lunch with Congresspeople Pat Schroeder (Democrat, Colorado), Lynne Woolsey (Democrat, California) and Cleo Fields (Democrat, Louisiana).

Running slightly late, they hurry through the wide, bright halls of the Capitol Building. Just as they arrive at Pat Schroeder's office, an alarm bell rings through the building. Ms. Schroeder does her best at introductions over the bell.

SCHROEDER: There's a great story of when the bells go off. There was a person here and the bells went off and they asked,

"What does that mean?" And someone said, "I don't know. I think some congressmen escaped." It actually means we have a vote. The abuse never ends.

CHERI: That's what it means?

SCHROEDER: Yeah. We have fifteen minutes to get our bodies down there. That means the house floor is going on and they're debating something. We're supposed to be listening on that TV over there. We can all read lips though, right?

FIELDS: There's also a beeper that goes off and tells you what bills we're voting on.

SCHROEDER: And then we have a research staff that knows where we come from, politically. They give us advice and pros and cons. There's so much going on and we all have our special interests.

CHERI: Well, I think it's great that you would meet with us. Where do we start? Okay, what's giving us trouble? Jobs . . . finding a job, education, health care . . .

WOOLSEY: I'm on the Education and Labor Committee, and we're working on jobs all the time. We're working on putting together a program where students in the eleventh and twelfth grade can start working while they're going to school, particularly students who aren't going to college. It's exciting, because a lot of young people are not finishing high school because they don't see any future. The work/study program changed this. How does that sound?

CHERI: That sounds about right.

FIELDS: Another problem along those lines is that many students who go to college graduate with loan debts that they can't

we are on the trip alone. Eileen and I went to the White House and drove in circles about six times while they filmed us. I was really frustrated—combo of things—tired, stressed due to self-imposed pressure and pissed off at the guys. Brad finally said that they wanted to leave town (but didn't want to say that on camera). Why must everything be an act? Who cares if the cameras were on? If the guys wanted to leave town they should have said so. I bitched to Eileen about Wade and Brad, then burst into tears. Of course, a camera was immediately in my face. As predicted, crying on national television. When we met back up with the guys, we aired our feelings. By the time we got into the car everything was settled. Wade is so sensitive to my feelings. (Almost too perfect—maybe he just knows how to play the game.)

afford to pay and they're bankrupt before they get their first job. This year we dealt with national service. You may be familiar with that. That's where students may perform services for the government before, during and after college to relieve their debt.

CHERI: So you guys have been thinking about this stuff. I'm relieved.

SCHROEDER: Oh, yeah. And it's more complicated than you may have thought. In the committee I chair on armed services, we're trying to deal with defense conversion. For the first time, as we dismantle parts of our defense industry, there's no place for those people to enter the civilian sector and retain those skills. If you take a guy who's been making nuclear submarines and you retrain him to run a restaurant, and then five years from now we need to make nuclear submarines again, we're in trouble. He's lost those skills. So what we're doing is trying to take the research and development that we paid for as taxpayers and start applying it. We're the best in the world at basic research, but then other countries come in and take the product and make it there and sell it back to us. So we're busy trying to figure out the conversion component that goes right to jobs.

WOOLSEY: Believe it or not, we think about health care, too. I have four kids. They're twenty-six to thirty-one years old. Three are college graduates and two of them still don't have health-care coverage. I just paid for some major dental work for my daughter. I'm glad to do it and I'm lucky that I can, but she's a college graduate and has a great job, but no health care.

SCHROEDER: I have two children and it's the same way. And a dog. He's not covered, either.

WOOLSEY: It's difficult to change things, though, because there's so much resistance. Everyone has their own interests and they fight tooth and nail to protect them. Clinton's plan isn't perfect, but I think it moves in the right direction and underlines the fact that things have to change.

SCHROEDER: Let me ask you guys a question. Why does your generation think we're not worth talking to?

Wade laughs nervously.

FIELDS: You guys are an exception, of course.

SCHROEDER: I seem to get farther from my children's friends. Do you look at it like, "Politics, that's something for your generation"?

CHERI: I think it's just that we feel so far away from everyone. It helps that Clinton's young. Like, he had Soul Asylum play the other night. That was great, because it ties things in. But how could we really relate to Bush? He was never going to concern himself with our issues.

FIELDS: I actually see a changing trend. I see more college students worried about deficit reduction because they're starting to see that who's really going to suffer is not the guys making decisions today, but them. In Louisiana, for instance, we have more college students registered to vote than any other state. That's because we have a very active voter-registration drive on college campuses. It's almost mandatory.

When you register for college, you also register to vote. A lot of my colleagues don't really pay attention to the youth agenda too much, but the more young people who are registered to vote, the more politicians will pay attention to your voice.

SCHROEDER: Congressman Fields feels the same way you do.

FIELDS: I'm the baby of the bunch.

CHERI: How old are you?

FIELDS: I was elected to Congress at twenty-nine. I was elected to the state senate at twenty-four.

CHERI: How did you get elected so young?

FIELDS: Basically, in college I was on the student government.

EILEEN: So am I.

FIELDS: It just shifts on to bigger things.

CHERI: I think we're all starting to panic a little. We see our paychecks dwindling after taxes are taken out and then you hear people say, "Well, you might not even receive Social Security." So, we're starting to feel like we have to do something about it.

WOOLSEY: This may sound a little defensive, but one of the reasons you think taxes are taking such a big part of your check is that your wages haven't grown over the last ten years. We've gone the wrong direction. A lot of people have gotten poorer, while a few have gotten very rich.

SCHROEDER: We've supported the defense of the world, and that's part of what you have

to pay for. Think about it. What we're
doing is providing defense for all these
countries that already have health care,
that don't have college tuition. They spend
their tax money on that and we spend our tax
money on them. It's a terrific deal, if you
think about it. You gotta figure . . . what
are the 250,000 American troops doing in
West Germany? They're protecting West Germany from East Germany, except now they're
all one country. It doesn't make much
sense.

BRAD: I'm not so sure we should let the
German army grow. It seems like racism is
on the rise over there . . . and in this
country, too. I've been reading too many
stories about hate crimes.

SCHROEDER: We're toughening the penalties
on hate crimes at the federal level. You're
absolutely right. I thought we'd never hear
some of the things we hear today. Sexism
is on the rise, too. This burning of clin-
ics and shooting of doctors . . . going
after people because of their race or religion . . . that is not America. I really
hope your generation can put a lot of that
to rest. On campuses, too, I hear it's
really gotten quite heavy. You must see
that in Georgia.

BRAD: Yeah. See, what I think it is in
Atlanta is that you have a lot of black universities and black private colleges. So
you have a younger generation of African-
American students that are well-read and
educated and they look back on Martin
Luther King's philosophy on dealing with
violence and they look at Malcolm X's philosophy—some of them sort of combine the
two, some go one way, and some go the other.

They feel frustrated. They're trying to better themselves and still there's all these little things.

SCHROEDER: Like what?

BRAD: You might be walking down the sidewalk and maybe a Caucasian lady is walking toward you and she'll cross to the other side of the street. Simple things like that are frustrating, and through frustration you have separation. So on a lot of college campuses, you even have separate student governments. The blacks are doing one thing, whites are doing another, and Asians and Hispanics are doing another. It seems to me that it would be better if everybody could work together.

The bell goes off, calling members of Congress to vote.

FIELDS: That means that we have to get going, but let me just thank you for the opportunity to sit and talk with you. It's always good to see individuals close to my age on the hill. My only challenge to you is to be true to your dreams. You can be anything you want to be as long as you're willing to pay the price and work hard. Thanks so much for coming up here to the hill.

SCHROEDER: Well, you have pizza to eat and we have votes to cast. Thanks for coming.

The members of Congress leave.

CHERI: I can't believe none of you would eat. The congresspeople and I were the only ones with the guts to eat.

The cast scarfs pizza in Pat Schroeder's office after meeting with congresspeople on Capitol Hill. TIFFANY HOSS

CUT TO:

EXTERIOR STREET—AFTERNOON

After their visit to the White House, Eileen and Cheri are waiting at the car for Brad and Wade.

CHERI: What bothers me is that they're not trying to help things. Wade's like, "I'm not interested in any issues, so I'm not gonna talk." That is so rude. These people are having us there . . .

EILEEN: I didn't think it was bad at all. I thought they were easy to talk to.

CHERI: To me that was so childish. Excuse me, Mr. Twenty-seven-year-old Maturity. If someone invites you to their house, you don't go and just not talk to them.

EILEEN: It wasn't like they were quizzing us . . .

CHERI: It's not about political things but, my god, it's part of his life. He does live here. Something must interest him. Thank god he's cute or he'd be nowhere.

Wade and Brad show up.

BRAD: (*to Cheri*) What upset you today?

CHERI: What upset me today? You guys didn't want to go talk to the congress-people and that's fine, but it was set up. If someone invites you to their house, you don't make a pact not to talk to them because you don't want to be there.

BRAD: I talked to them.

CHERI: I know, but before we went in there, you guys said, "We're not going to talk."

WADE: That was just a joke. Do you take everything we say seriously?

CHERI: Did you say anything?

WADE: I didn't have anything to say. I was nervous. Not because I said I wasn't going to say anything. And regardless of whether I said anything or not, why should you worry about it?

CHERI: Because Eileen's quiet to start with. I knew she wasn't going to say anything. Then you guys say that you're not going to say anything, so I just feel like it's up to me. And that's fine. That didn't bother me so much. Then, afterward, we're like, "What are we going to do?" And you would not say anything. We were totally in the dark. It's like pulling teeth with you guys to find out what's going on.

BRAD: I didn't think it was necessary to explain everything at the time. I didn't think we needed to get into it.

CHERI: I just feel like I have to carry things.

BRAD: But you don't have to carry anything. The way me and Wade act isn't your responsibility.

CHERI: But it's not just that. It was the whole culmination of things that came to a head when I wanted to find out what was going on and you guys wouldn't talk.

WADE: I thought all we needed to know was that you guys were going to your place, we were going to ours, and we'd meet at four-thirty. That's it.

CHERI: Well, we have to communicate better. We thought things had changed or whatever.

WADE: Well, we have to communicate better, then.

CHERI: Fine.

BRAD: It's clarified. I mean I'm clear. Are y'all clear? If you ain't clear . . . I don't like static. If anyone's got something to say, say it now. Get it off your chest. This is confession . . . come down to the altar and get it out there. Eileen, you got a problem? You're not going to get in the car and start hitting me, are you?

EILEEN: No. Don't be silly.

CHERI: We all have been irritable, but I felt the pressure.

BRAD: That's fine, but you took the pressure on yourself. We didn't put pressure on you.

CHERI: I'm not blaming you.

BRAD: Thank you. That's all I wanted to know. Let's go to Virginia!

Motel 6, Roanoke—Wade called me from his room to say good night.

DAY 5:

TRAVEL: 391 miles/8 hours raw drive time

PLACES OF INTEREST:
- Before you leave Roanoke, you may want to check out **Miniature Graceland**. Don and Kim Epperly have dedicated their front yard to a tiny rendering of The King's homestead. Included is a performance hall where a Ken-doll Elvis performs for an equally inanimate audience. 601 Riverland Road.
- **Cornelia State Prison**. Brad's dad has agreed to run you by the maximum security corrections facility where he works.

PLACES TO EAT:
- **Brad's house**. Loosen up those belts. Brad's mom is going to cook us up a Southern feast.
- **Majestic Diner** in Atlanta is perfect for either post-clubbing tonight or pre-road tomorrow. 1031 Ponce De Leon Avenue.

NIGHTLIFE:
- **Five Points** is likened to Haight-Ashbury and is home to small rock venues like **The Point** (420 Moreland Avenue) and **The Star** (437 Moreland Avenue). In keeping with an Elvis theme for the day, the latter houses a shrine to The King.
- **The Chameleon Club** in Buckhead pulls in the frat-type college crowd. 3179 Peachtree Road. (404)261-8004.
- For hip-hop, Southern style, visit **Club Garage** at 580 Whitehall Street. (404)222-0959.
- **Homage Coffee House** offers a less potent, but certainly more stimulating spin on the evening. 255 Trinity Avenue SW. (404)681-2662.

ACCOMMODATIONS:
Another **Motel 6**, this time in Decatur, Georgia.
2565 Wesley Chapel Road. (404)288-6911.

FADE IN:
EXTERIOR PHONE BOOTH—MORNING

After a big country breakfast at a greasy
diner in Roanoke, Brad finds a phone and
calls his parents.

BRAD: Hey, it's Brad.

DAD: Hey boy, where you at?

BRAD: I'm in Virginia somewhere.

DAD: Y'all comin' for dinner tonight?

BRAD: Yeah. That's why I was callin' Mama,
to make sure she was ready.

DAD: What time will y'all be by?

BRAD: Somewhere between one and two.
What's Mama makin'?

DAD: She said she's gonna have turkey with
dressing, green beans, glorious macaroni—
you know, her special macaroni. All that.
It's gonna be terrific. Homemade rolls . . .

BRAD: How about dessert?

DAD: She's gonna make some of that cherry
pie she's been making. You know that one?

BRAD: Yeah. Okay.

DAD: All right now, you take care of yourself and we'll see you later.

> Roanoke is a cool small town—lots of old ads like "Enjoy Coca-Cola" painted on the sides of buildings.

CUT TO:

INTERIOR NEON—MORNING

Back on the road, our travelers make time to Georgia.

CHERI: I miss school.

EILEEN: Really?

CHERI: I was ready to get out when I got out. I was sick of it. But now I'm ready to go back.

BRAD: I don't think I'll ever miss school. Soon as I graduate I'm gonna get as far away from school as I can.

EILEEN: I like it a lot.

CHERI: I had a blast.

WADE: How long have you been out?

CHERI: Since December of '90.

BRAD: Damn, I was just getting out of high school then. You're old. When I was a senior in high school, I wanted to go to Morehouse College in Atlanta. It's an all-black male college, supposed to be the best in the country. I wanted to go there, but then I started thinking . . . I went to Morehouse and walked around the campus. It's all black professors, all black people, and it's right there in the A.U. Center. You got Morehouse, which is an all-black male college, and right next to it you got Spelman, which is an all-black female college and then you got Clark Atlanta which is all-black coed. So in that whole campus area, no whites come in at all. And coming from Habersham, it was refreshing to be around so many blacks,

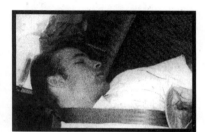

Wade catches up on some sleep on the way to Atlanta. EILEEN CHUNG

Up extra early so we could all work out. The guys left without me so I jogged to the gym. Hilarious! There were fifteen black guys and me riding stationary bikes and watching Oprah on some homosexual topic—everyone was yelling at the TV.

especially intelligent blacks. But it got monotonous real quick because it seemed like they all had a chip on their shoulder against every other race.

EILEEN: Yeah, that can happen.

BRAD: That's not what I wanted to happen. I thought it over and talked to some of my white friends and they were like, "If that's what you want to do, go to Morehouse. But we just don't want you to come back with an attitude." A lot of the guys from Morehouse and girls from Spelman have a real bad attitude. They don't need any kind of outside influence. And, see, a lot of them come from inner-city schools which were just about all black—then they go to an all-black college. I just think they're not going to be prepared for the outside world. You can't go to a workplace that's all black.

EILEEN: That's so isolated. I mean, it's great to be interested in your culture and everything, but you need to have friends of all different backgrounds.

CHERI: It's strange, because in St. Louis there isn't much of an Asian population. Or Mexican or whatever. In St. Louis you're either black or white. So if you're Chinese you're white. One of my friends was Mexican. She was white. St. Louis is very racially divided. The north is all black and the south is all white.

BRAD: That's weird. In Cornelia, Laotians and Asians are black. If something were to go down racially in the county, Mexicans, Asians, and blacks would all band together against the whites every time. You got a few Asians they call wannabes, 'cause they

It's strange driving without music. Because of copyright laws, songs in the background of our conversations could get expensive. Here and there we're allowed to listen to music. The first time we were given half an hour of music, we fought the whole time. Brad put a tape in, which we all soon rejected. Couldn't get any music on the radio, so I told Wade to pick one of my tapes. Brad made noise so that we couldn't hear the music. He said he felt insulted that we had rejected his tape. I was pissed so we had it out. I told him that he was being immature. "Grow up!" I yelled. Anyway, we wasted our whole music period by fighting about it. Eileen doesn't say much— she just watches everything. Wade will say a word or two, but usually it's just Brad and me arguing.

wannabe white so bad, but most of them you'll see hanging around with blacks.

EILEEN: The worst are when . . . have you seen it when they try to dye their hair? I mean, it's not going to be blond. It's black hair. I mean, they try to dye it, and it's orange and it's hideous. It's not going to be blond. You can go out and get green contacts or blue contacts—you're still going to have dark hair and dark eyes. Get real.

BRAD: But those Asians are black. My friend Raz, he just hangs with the brothers. You'll see him in my neighborhood just hangin'.

CHERI: In St. Louis my brother got pulled over in South County, which is the white area, in the parking lot of a mall because he was with a black guy. And the black guy was really nice looking. So they got pulled over for turning the wrong way in a parking garage. Who gets pulled over in a parking lot? They were frisked and everything, just because a black guy was with a white guy and the white guy had long hair. That's just the way St. Louis is.

CUT TO:

INTERIOR NEON—AFTERNOON

Brad is driving as the Neon rolls into Habersham County, Georgia. The day is warm and the sun is shining.

BRAD: We're real close. That's the high school right up there. We're about five miles from my house. This is where I got my first speeding ticket, right here. I was doing about ninety-eight on this road right here. He pulled me over right there.

CHERI: First time I got a ticket, I had my license like two weeks. I was steering and my girlfriend was doing the gas. No, wait, she was steering and I was doing the gas. I got pulled over.

BRAD: I had a fuzzbuster sitting on the dash, had the t-tops off that Iroc . . . there was nothing I could do.

CHERI: You were driving an Iroc?

BRAD: I was going ninety-eight on this road right here, just winding that sucker out.

CHERI: You do live in the boonies.

EILEEN: There are so many cows out here.

BRAD: Lot of cows, but more chickens.

WADE: Ever go cow-tipping?

BRAD: Yeah.

EILEEN: Awwwww!

CHERI: Are we going to?

BRAD: If we were staying here tonight we could.

EILEEN: Nooo! It kills them!

BRAD AND WADE: It kills them!? No it doesn't!

EILEEN: Yes, it does. They can't get up and they have heart attacks and die.

WADE: How do you know? You've never been around cows.

BRAD: It does not kill them. Believe me, I cow-tip all the time. They sleep standing up. You just push them over and run like hell. 'Cause they'll chase you. They can move. Wade's gonna find that out when he rides that bull.

CUT TO:

EXTERIOR PRISON—AFTERNOON

After arriving at Brad's house and meeting his parents and friends, Brad, Cheri, Wade, and Brad's father, Lafayette, tour Cornelia. Eileen stays at Brad's house to help his mother with dinner.

The tour of Brad's town ends up at the Cornelia State Prison, where Lafayette works.

Brad's street is half middle-class, half poverty-stricken. Two separate worlds on the same block. Seems strange that while Brad is going to college, striving toward a career as a cop, guys on his block are making a career out of drug sales. I could sense the animosity of the onlookers as we were parked at the poorer end of his street. Brad said that he would not be safe in that area if we weren't with him.

LAFAYETTE: This is one place that you guys never want to end up. I've been here twenty-one years. This is a maximum security institution. This place houses murderers, robbers, kidnappers, rapists, everything.

WADE: Where are they all at right now?

LAFAYETTE: Right here . . . in this dormitory, the cell blocks. They're only allowed out basically one time a day for recreation. They're locked down twenty-three hours a day. They don't come out for any reason unless they have an appointment with a doctor or an attorney. Other than that, he's in a one-man cell for twenty-three hours a day. Can you imagine that? Doing five years? The pressure? Now that's the one building over there, SMU, Special Management Unit. Back behind there there's more regular dormitory living.

WADE: What gets you in SMU?

LAFAYETTE: Well, you break the rules or you ask for protective custody. Some of these guys might feel their life is in danger in the regular population and they ask for protective custody. Then they get locked down in SMU for thirty days. After that we review their case, look at it real hard, and ask them if they want to go back to population.

WADE: What do they need protection from?

LAFAYETTE: Stabbing. That goes on sometimes.

CHERI: How do they get knives?

LAFAYETTE: They make them over there in the shop and smuggle them back inside. See, there's a shortage of men. I only have two eyes and I can't watch everybody all the time.

WADE: How many guards are there on, like, recreation time?

LAFAYETTE: Two. Two guards watching thirty, thirty-five, forty inmates. Two officers are watching.

BRAD: But they don't carry guns.

LAFAYETTE: That's true. There are no guns inside the institution. All we have are radios and sometimes a nightstick. That's all we have as our defense.

WADE: Do you ever get attacked?

LAFAYETTE: Sure. Sometimes it happens. Not often. As long as we keep them under control it doesn't happen too often. Sometimes, though, he gets angry; he gets mad and jumps on somebody. Most of them are young strong men like you. I'm fifty years old. I can't wrestle them always.

WADE: How come it doesn't happen more? I

mean, if he's in there for twenty years and you don't have a gun, he's got nothing to lose.

LAFAYETTE: But we have power over him. The court has given him to us for a certain amount of time. Plus we have a disciplinary committee here that will give him more time if he slips up. Someone in here for three years can be out in one year on good behavior. If he assaults me, he's in here for three years. Normally, it works pretty good on them.

CHERI: Does it bother you that they might commit a heinous crime and get sentenced for twenty years and only do five?

LAFAYETTE: No. I don't take this job personally. I don't know what he's here for. Quite frankly, I don't want to know. To me he's just another inmate. He's not black, he's not white, he's not polka dot. He's an inmate. And there are some people here for heinous crimes.

WADE: Wouldn't it help you to know so you know who might be more dangerous?

LAFAYETTE: I can't. I can't be afraid here. If I ever do, I'll turn my badge in. When I come in these doors I can't be afraid. If I was I couldn't work here. I have to be in charge. You guys don't ever want to be in there. You have no idea what this place is from the outside here. You couldn't imagine what it's like. Jason, the bad man, Jason, he's in there right now and men like him. And he's not afraid of anything or anybody.

> Tonight I cried again. I cry so easily lately. Wade must think I'm a basket case. Much of this emotion is due to the Matt situation. I promised myself that I would break up with him when I got home. It weighs heavily on my mind. Although I try to put those thoughts aside, they linger in my subconscious. Therefore, little disappointments have a larger impact than they normally would.

CUT TO:

INTERIOR NEON—NIGHT

After a huge country meal, the gang packs up and gets on the road to Atlanta proper.

CHERI: (*to Eileen*) So what were you talking about with Brad's friends?

EILEEN: (*to Brad*) What was that? You were the only one who wanted to light a fire? You were afraid of a little jumping mouse?

WADE: What's the story behind that?

BRAD: My friends run their mouths too much.

EILEEN: You know how Brad's not scared of anything? Well, when he went camping before this trip, he went with his buddies and it turns out Brad's really scared of bears. They were getting ready for bed and getting ready to put out the fire. So he gathered all the wood he could find and built a big fire so the light would scare away the bears. And then he kept hearing noises, but it turned out it was just this little jumping mouse, but it scared him.

Brad huddles with friends during a quick stopover at his house in Cornelia, GA. EILEEN CHUNG

BRAD: See, I wanted the fire because it was cold and we didn't string up our food and stuff, and I didn't want bears and raccoons tearing apart my backpack and all that. That's what that was. And we were all sitting on this log when this jumping mouse jumped behind me. I didn't even say anything until they said something. I just jumped because they jumped.

EILEEN: What else? Oh his mom told me something about chicken bones. When he was little, he used to go into the garbage and eat chicken bones.

BRAD: I was just a baby.

EILEEN: I know, but it was cute.

FADE OUT.

DAY 6:

TRAVEL: 367 miles/7.4 hours raw drive time

Roll those watches back an hour. You cross into Central Time on your way to Lynchburg.

PLACES OF INTEREST:
- **Confederama**, in Chattanooga, is a miniature recreation of the Civil War, complete with five thousand toy soldiers fighting it out to the death. A strobing light show will give you a feel for the original *Apocalypse Now*. 3742 Tennessee Avenue. (615)821-2812.
- **Jack Daniel's Distillery**, the nation's oldest distillery. Jack was an old bootlegger. Lynchburg, Tennessee, on Highway 55. (615)428-9488.
- The city of **Oak Ridge**, Tennessee, was established in 1942 as a manufacturing point for weapons-grade uranium used in the bombs dropped on Hiroshima and Nagasaki. The government didn't admit its existence until 1949. It's now an ecological disaster.
- **The Farm** in Summertown, Tennessee, was established as a spiritual collective (basically, a commune) in 1971. The inhabitants went through some rough economic times, almost ending in bankruptcy in 1983. Today, roughly three hundred residents operate a school, clinic, store, bakery, and soy dairy. They welcome visitors, especially if you buy some of their vegetarian foods or a T-shirt. 100 Farm Road. (615)964-3574.

PLACES TO EAT:
Chattanooga:
- **Cahoots Restaurant** once served as the town's jail. Now it serves up burgers, etc. Book 'em, Dano. In Fayetteville; (615)433-1173.
Memphis:
- **Buntyn**, a great Southern cafe next to the railroad tracks and a feed store. 3070 Southern

Today was to be _our_ day. We had complained to the producer that we wanted more freedom. So ... we were given the drive time, told that we had to make it to Memphis tonight and handed a Let's Go, USA guide. We could stop anywhere we wanted to. We were in charge. At first we didn't handle it so well. The guys slept while I read to Eileen, who was driving. We passed all kinds of possible stops, and when we chose a lunch destination, we didn't realize that it was hours away.

Avenue. (901)458-8776.
- **Beale Street** (home of the blues) is lined with
places to eat. (901)526-0110.
- **Charlie Vergos Rendezvous** specializes in dry,
spiced ribs. 52 South Second Street. (901)523-2746.
- **Payne's** used to be a filling station. Try the pork
sandwich. 1762 Lamar Avenue. (902)272-1523.

NIGHTLIFE:
Memphis:
- **B. B. King's Blues Club** on Beale Street was new in
1991, but is already the name blues club in the
city. (901)524-5464.
- **Rum Boogie Cafe**, also on Beale, is one of the
street's most crowded venues. (901)528-0150.
- If the tourist scene is getting you down, try **The
Antenna Club**. The doorman requests two forms of I.D.
and dirt under your fingernails. 1588 Madison
Avenue. (901)276-4052.

ACCOMMODATIONS:
- **Motel 6**, 1117 East Brooks Road, Memphis.
(901) 346-0992.
- **Elvis Motel**. The Days Inn across from Graceland
sports Elvis memorabilia and a guitar-shaped swimming pool. 3839 Elvis Presley Boulevard. (901)346-
5500.

FADE IN:
INTERIOR NEON—MORNING

Eileen takes the wheel for the long road to
Memphis.

EILEEN: So, Brad, how did it go with
Chrissy last night?

BRAD: Everything went good up to a certain
point.

EILEEN: What point?

BRAD: I was just snapping at her for
everything.

EILEEN: So things aren't good?

BRAD: No, everything's fine between me and her. I gave her my beaded necklace last night.

EILEEN: What beaded necklace?

BRAD: The one I've been wearing the whole trip. That's real symbolic. If I give a girl my beaded necklace, that's like putting my brand on 'em.

EILEEN: Putting your WHAT on them?

BRAD: Uh, oh. I said the wrong thing, didn't I?

EILEEN: Yeah. You make it sound like cattle or pigs or something.

WADE: It just means it's his special girl.

CHERI: We're gonna be close to my house when we get to Memphis. It's only six hours. We can take a six-hour jog in our free time.

WADE: Oh, man, listen to this (*he reads a letter in an advice column from an issue of* Cosmopolitan) "I've been sharing an apartment with another woman for about six months. Last week I came home from work and heard strange noises coming from the bathroom. When I opened the door, I found my roommate having sex with a girl who she told me was her best friend. I never thought she was a lesbian, just figured she was too busy to date. I'm very much against homosexuality and don't know what to do."

BRAD: Heh, heh! That would be something to see. If they were friends before she knew she was a lesbian, that shouldn't change their friendship any. That's what I think about it. If you had a friend and you found

> The more I get to know Wade, the more I'm attracted to him. On the one hand, he seems so mature and together, especially in dealing with women. On the other hand, he has a totally childlike side and acts goofy and fun. I think I should be more skeptical.

out he was a homosexual, there's no reason to stop being his friend.

EILEEN: Yeah. Exactly. It's not like they're going to hit on you.

BRAD: If they were going to, they would have by now.

WADE: (*reading another letter*) "I'm twenty-four and reasonably attractive, but overweight. The problem is that I'm still a virgin, which makes me feel like a freak. I'd really like to have sex, just to see what I've been missing. And I have some good male friends who I could probably sleep with whenever I'm ready, but I think I deserve better. When the right man comes along, how will I explain my years of celibacy?"

CHERI: Why would you have to explain virginity?

BRAD: I know that most men I know would like it.

EILEEN: Actually, a lot of guys I know would, too. But, I think it's weird because guys want to fool around but want to marry a virgin.

BRAD: That's exactly true.

CHERI: I think that's changing, though. It's so unrealistic.

WADE: Yeah. It's old hat.

BRAD: Still, most of my friends, when we're talking, they'll say, "I would like my wife to be a virgin or to have slept with as few people as possible." The ideal thing would be to find a virgin.

Brad and I fight like brother and sister. We both are very argumentative and thrive on verbal challenge. I think this annoys Wade.

CHERI: You're gonna keep looking for a long time.

EILEEN: It's not fair to think that. If guys can, why can't girls?

BRAD: The ideal thing is to find a good-looking girl who's a virgin. That's the kind of girl that you hang on to and marry.

EILEEN: That's unfair, because they've been through the same things you have.

BRAD: And that's why you don't find many attractive virgins. You're an exception. But you don't find many attractive girls who are virgins, because most of them have been hit on so many times and messed with so much, they gave in at one time or another.

EILEEN: It's not necessarily "giving in." It's the same thing as with guys. Maybe she wanted it. It's not like they're giving in if they want it.

BRAD: I'm just saying that more attractive girls have had more opportunity to have sex and don't have excuses for why they haven't. Ugly girls can say, "Well, I don't have anything but losers hitting on me." But attractive girls have attractive guys hitting on them. That makes it all the more attractive, because they're attracted to them. If you got a bunch of ugly guys, it's pretty easy to remain a virgin. I haven't met many attractive virgins.

EILEEN: Have you asked a lot of people, though? I think you'd be surprised at how many people are virgins.

BRAD: I knew a virgin who was hot . . .

EILEEN: Listen to that. He talks about it like it's a dinosaur.

I'm not really sure how Eileen feels. She really has been clammed-up. In our one-on-one discussions, I realize that Eileen is usually very talkative and bubbly. She doesn't know why she's crawled into a shell. I think part of it has to do with our ages and our personalities—with Wade and me being several years older and Brad and me being somewhat overbearing, Eileen has taken a back seat to the three of us.

Cheri and Brad take a roadside time-out on the way to Memphis. EILEEN CHUNG

CHERI: Are we staying at the Elvis Motel tonight?

BRAD: Elvis Motel, Lord have mercy.

WADE: Maybe we should get a Ouija board and call him back.

EILEEN: Have you guys ever played with a Ouija board?

CHERI: Yeah.

EILEEN: It's really weird. It's like, nobody's pushing it . . .

BRAD: Aww, people are pushing it, they just don't admit it.

CHERI: It's dangerous, though, if you really get it working.

EILEEN: It really is.

WADE: You really believe in Ouija boards?

CHERI: Yeah.

WADE: How is it dangerous? I don't believe in that.

CHERI: You can call evil spirits into your house . . .

EILEEN: And they won't go away.

CHERI: Because you called them in and they're locked there.

BRAD: You're gonna tell me that y'all are Catholics and you believe in your religion, but still you believe in Ouija boards.

CHERI: Yeah. Why not?

BRAD: You can't do that.

CHERI: There's spirits. We believe in purgatory. Maybe those people are in purgatory.

BRAD: You can do it, but it's wrong.

EILEEN: Hey! Where do you get off? Catholics believe in purgatory.

WADE: You really think those Ouija boards work?

CHERI: Yeah, if you know what you're doing. Most people just fool around with them. My girlfriend used to be really into witchcraft and everything . . . and it can be dangerous if you know what you're doing and you call spirits.

WADE: So your friend who practiced witchcraft, what happened to her? Did she get haunted or something?

CHERI: No, but she had another friend . . . she got out of it because it was dangerous. But she has stories. One of her aunts practices witchcraft, so they're sort of in the circle of people who do it and they've had friends who get spirits who won't leave.

WADE: It's easy to scare yourself. You're alone, it's dark . . .

BRAD: I'm more afraid of real people. I believe more in the harm a real person can do. Like my dad was telling y'all about the Jasons and Freddy Krugers in that prison back there . . . that's the real boogeyman that I'm worried about. I don't believe in the rest of it. If y'all want to, we can go out and get a Ouija board and go have a séance at pitch midnight.

EILEEN: See, I'm not into that. I don't

One of the many reminders that you are in the Bible Belt. SAM JONES

like Ouija boards. I'm just saying that . . .

CHERI: I stay away from them.

BRAD: You're scared of them?

EILEEN: No . . . I just think you're dealing with something you don't know much about.

CHERI: It's like mixing a bunch of chemicals when you don't know what the end result is going to be.

BRAD: So that's the reason you don't mix chemicals, because you're afraid of what the end result might be. Correct?

CHERI: That's why you don't play with a Ouija board, because you don't know what the end result might be.

BRAD: So you're afraid of the end result. Right?

CHERI: Right.

BRAD: Thus saying you're afraid of the powers of the Ouija board. Correct?

EILEEN: You're making it sound like we're really into witchcraft.

BRAD: It just seems to me that you fear witchcraft, which is weird to me because I don't.

EILEEN: At the same time, Brad, that's just you. You don't think you're afraid of anything . . . although you won't go skydiving, you don't like jumping mice, and you don't like bears.

BRAD: Hold on. Time out. There's a difference between being cautious about skydiving and being afraid.

EILEEN: I won't go skydiving, either, but I'll come right out and say it, that I'm afraid.

BRAD: But I'm not scared of it. If it came down to it, I would skydive. But I don't see the point in putting myself in the way of unnecessary harm.

EILEEN: That's the way I feel about a Ouija board.

BRAD: You can compare it to a Ouija board, but I know people have died skydiving. It's on the news that people have died skydiving. Parachutes have not opened. That's mechanical. I just believe in human error. But I'm not afraid of the act. It's like playing Russian roulette.

CHERI: So what's your point?

EILEEN: There's nothing wrong with being afraid of something.

BRAD: I know there's nothing wrong with it, but I'm not.

CHERI: So you're just manipulating the definition of fear.

BRAD: I'm not manipulating the definition of fear.

CHERI: You don't choose to put yourself in the way of unnecessary harm, but the point is that you're afraid that something would happen to you when you jump out of that airplane. Correct?

BRAD: It's not fear. I just don't care enough about skydiving to put myself in that danger. I do other things that are probably more dangerous than skydiving, but I like doing them. I'll go out on a rainy night and drive a car as fast as it will go

We had adjoining rooms in the Elvis Motel, but Brad locked the door in between. I think that if he can't have Eileen, then he wants me to have nothing to do with Wade. His immaturity drives me nuts.

on a winding road, but I love that. I just don't think I'd like skydiving enough to put myself in the danger.

EILEEN: I think you think you're less manly or less masculine if you're afraid of something. It's okay to be afraid of something. It's okay to cry.

WADE: Sometimes I watch *Brian's Song* just to bawl.

BRAD: You actually cry at a movie, man?

EILEEN: Brad, for example, is one of those guys that I'm talking about.

BRAD: Serious. You cry at a movie?

WADE: Hell yeah. I'm not like *boo-hoo-hoo* . . . but I've got tears coming down my face.

BRAD: Oh, man.

CHERI: *Brian's Song*, what's that?

WADE: It's a true story. It's about Gale Sayers and this guy Brian Piccolo. James Caan plays Brian Piccolo. He gets cancer and he dies. It's back in the late sixties, early seventies. Gale Sayers was one of the greatest black running backs . . . greatest running backs, period. And Brian Piccolo is white and they become best friends, even though it shouldn't really be that way. Then Brian Piccolo gets cancer and he dies and man, it's sad.

BRAD: Yeah, that's a trip, man.

EILEEN: I didn't see it, but I heard it was a total tearjerker.

CHERI: *Beaches* was just like me and my best friend . . . exactly.

EILEEN: So many people have told me that.

BRAD: Something would have to bother me a whole lot for me to cry. If I did cry it would be by myself. I wouldn't cry in front of anyone, especially my girlfriend.

EILEEN: Why especially your girlfriend?

BRAD: I just know she couldn't look at me in the same light. She'd always look at me as being weaker.

CHERI: Oh, God. You'll grow out of that, hopefully.

EILEEN: Just for the record, I don't think any girl would think you're weaker because you cry.

CHERI: Me neither.

BRAD: Man, let me out of here. It's getting too emotional. I'm gonna start getting sensitive.

FADE OUT.

DAY 7:

Saturday, October 2:

Memphis, TN, to Clarksdale, MS

TRAVEL: 214 miles/4.2 hours raw drive time

PLACES OF INTEREST:
Memphis:
- **Graceland,** need I say more? 3734 Elvis Presley
Boulevard. (901)332-3322.
- **Shangri-La Records** on Madison is the best record
store in the city. 1916 Madison Avenue. (901)274-
1916.
- **National Civil Rights Museum,** near Beale Street,
is located at the assassination site of Dr. Martin
Luther King, Jr. 450 Mulberry Street. (901) 521-
9699.
- **Beale Street Historic District** is tourist cen-
tral. Several blocks of upscale clubs, restaurants,
and gift shops. 168 Beale Street. (901)526-0110.

→ **DEMOLITION DERBY.** Draw straws . . . the loser gets
behind the wheel of a Detroit dinosaur and smashes
it to pieces. Last car still rolling takes the
prize. What else are you gonna do with a '71 station
wagon? The derbies and mud drag races run every
other Saturday night at Dave McKinney's track in
Bolivar, Tennessee.

- **Scenic Drive.** On the way out of Memphis take
historic Highway 61 south through the Mississippi
Delta for a look at the roots of the blues. "Yes, I
think it can be quite easily done . . ."

PLACES TO EAT:
- **See Memphis.**
- Grab a dog at the demolition derby.

- **Lebanese Rest Haven,** 419 South State Street,
Clarksdale, Mississippi.

ACCOMMODATIONS:
- **The Beacon Inn,** 1910 State Street, Clarksdale,
Mississippi. (601)624-4391.

FADE IN:
INTERIOR NEON—DAY

A gray, drizzling sky hangs over Memphis as
the cast departs from Graceland, where they
toured the home of The King and dutifully
signed the stone wall surrounding the
grounds of the mansion.

Wade steers the Neon toward the National
Civil Rights Museum, located in a run-down
neighborhood not far from the trendy
tourist strip of Beale Street.

CHERI: So, who thinks Elvis is still
alive?

WADE: I do. He was in my room last night.

CHERI: Is that what all that noise was?

WADE: Yeah.

EILEEN: That place was amazing. Everything
around there is a total shrine to Elvis.

WADE: What's amazing is how popular he
became so fast. I mean, it's incredible.
Before he even went into the army he was a
total celebrity.

BRAD: What's amazing is how popular most
people get after they die. Same thing with
Bruce Lee. He got popular after he died.
Elvis, too. He was already a star, but it

Elvis Presley's Graceland mansion was his tribute to his success and his upbringing. The question remains: Is he really buried out back, or will he return to fill his sequined outfit once more? EILEEN CHUNG

just got to the point where he was an idol after he died.

CHERI: Look at the place he lived. He had to have so much imagination to make that whole thing.

EILEEN: A different personality in every room.

WADE: It was cool that he gave so much, too—$50,000 every month. Or was it every year?

BRAD: Every year at Christmas.

WADE: Every Christmas, $50,000. And didn't use it as a tax write-off.

EILEEN: He bought all these cars, too. He just walked into a dealer and bought thirty-one cars and just gave them away to family and friends, people on the street.

CHERI: I wish I had been walking down the street that day.

WADE: He would have to rent out a mall or a movie theater, you know, after everyone had gone . . . he would rent it out so that he could go shopping or see a movie. He couldn't do it during the day.

CHERI: The sad thing, though, is that he was always so concerned about being in the limelight and losing it . . . starting to fall. But it ruined him. Man, that room with the couch in it . . .

EILEEN: The jungle room?

CHERI: No, the yellow one.

WADE: Those rooms would be so sweet now if you just changed the colors . . . painted that yellow, like black or something . . .

EILEEN: No way. That yellow was great . . .

so seventies. That big chair looked so neat . . . mirrors everywhere.

CHERI: I hope the pictures turn out.

WADE: You can tell we're in the black part of town. You know why?

BRAD: Liquor stores?

WADE: Nope. Billboards. Look at that . . . every one of them. Isn't that weird? They only have the black people in the black part of town. Why don't they put them in other areas?

BRAD: Because, shit, y'all won't buy it.

EILEEN: What?

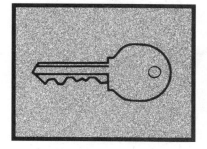

BRAD: Black models and stuff just sell to the black public a lot of the time. There's a few exceptions, but that's the general rule. That's the reason that Malavai Washington is ranked tenth in the world in tennis, but he can't get a tennis shoe endorsement.

WADE: Who's this now?

BRAD: A black tennis player. He can't get an endorsement because blacks don't play that much tennis and whites aren't going to buy Adidas just because he's endorsing them. Or, if he's endorsing Adidas and Agassi is endorsing Nike, whites will buy Nikes, even though a lot of the time he's ranked higher than Agassi. Same thing with Michael Chang.

EILEEN: Yeah, I was reading something about that.

BRAD: I never noticed it until I came home one day from high school and put a Brian Bosworth poster on the wall. My father came in and tore that sucker down.

WADE: Why?

BRAD: He said, "You go out and get your Bo Jackson poster or Herschel Walker poster. We've got enough trouble trying to get endorsements without you helping the other side."

WADE: That's bad.

BRAD: It makes sense, though. Because if I'm not helping to endorse them . . .

WADE: Yeah, but you like whoever you happen to like.

BRAD: But when I buy a poster, my money is going somewhere and being accounted for.

CHERI: See, I think it's attitudes like that that keep racism going.

BRAD: But, as a minority, you have to have that attitude some of the time, because the majority, which is Caucasian, have that attitude. Even though they might not express it all the time, it's shown, it figures.

EILEEN: It's true that advertising ignores minorities, but that's changing. That's why, like, *Self* magazine is starting this new section, "Global Beauty," which is paying attention to new makeup lines that suit other than Caucasian faces. It's still there. I mean, in Boston it's something like forty percent minority and they are totally ignored in advertising. But as far as the poster thing goes, I think you should put up whoever you want. You're making color an issue.

CHERI: It's like putting a chip on your shoulder.

BRAD: It's not a chip on my shoulder. It's

just helping my brothers. Nobody else is gonna help them, so I'm gonna help them. If I'm gonna spend five dollars on a poster, I might as well put it in Herschel Walker's pocket.

CHERI: Like he needs it.

BRAD: Like Brian Bosworth needs it. It's all about self-help. You cannot understand it and you probably won't understand it.

CHERI: I won't, because if you're basing what you do around your color, I think you're focusing on it more than we are.

BRAD: But what I'm saying is that you do it subconsciously and don't know you're doing it. You focus on color and you don't even know it because that's just the way you've always done it. I'm not saying it's bad, you just do it.

WADE: There's always going to be that kind of gap as long as that stuff goes on.

BRAD: And it's always gonna go on. So there's always going to be that gap.

No one in the car denies this.

CUT TO:

EXTERIOR CIVIL RIGHTS MUSEUM—DAY

The National Civil Rights Museum in Memphis is a beautiful modern building at the site of the Lorraine Motel, where Martin Luther King, Jr., was assassinated. Just a few blocks from the upscale tourist row of Beale Street, the structure stands in contrast to an uninspiring neighborhood.

The rain has stopped, but the sky is still threatening as the cast exits the museum.

Met a homeless woman who lives, in protest of the Martin Luther King museum, in a shack across the street. We had an argument with her that led me into a major argument with Brad. Brad doesn't realize that he probably is the only black man with whom I have ever had very close contact. In St. Louis, if you see a black man, you know he doesn't belong there because no blacks live in our parish. I try to be sensitive to the hardships Afro-Americans deal with due to their color, but sometimes I feel that they hide behind their color and blame race as a cause for all their problems.

BRAD: That was very interesting. Very interesting.

Across the street, they spot Jacqueline Smith, a lean, handsome black woman who has been living on the street across from the museum for five years. She is holding a sign that reads, "Boycott Civil Wrongs Museum."

BRAD: Y'all want to go talk to her?

WADE: I know you do.

They approach the small, dilapidated couch where Jacqueline lives. A pale blue tarp is suspended above it to keep out the rain. Seeing the cast approach, she rises to greet them.

BRAD: Hi. How are you?

JACQUELINE: Hi. I'm Jacqueline Smith.

BRAD: Brad Gober.

They all introduce themselves.

BRAD: I just wanted to know your reasons for boycotting this museum.

Jacqueline begins a well-rehearsed explanation. Her voice is confident and intelligent.

JACQUELINE: I've been living here for five and a half years in protest of the exploitation of Dr. King and the Lorraine Motel. I believe that in commemorating Dr. King, the Lorraine should be used for housing or some other way to help the disadvantaged. Two months before Dr. King's assassination, he preached a final sermon. In that sermon he said he did not want to be

remembered because he won the Nobel Peace
Prize. He said he wanted it to be remembered that he tried to live his life serv-
ing others; that he tried to feed the
hungry, clothe the unclothed. Therefore, I
think the Lorraine should be used in some
way to reflect his wishes. Why not have a job
center or community college or something
related more directly to helping this community? Also, look at this neighborhood.
You see the building of the Civil Rights
Museum in this community . . . it's all part
of a land-grabbing conspiracy. They are
taking land from the poor people and using
the gentrification process. The poor people
are being priced out of their roots. Eventually, I believe the Lorraine will be surrounded by condominiums and town houses. I
feel the greatest honor we can bestow upon
Dr. King is to commemorate him by continu-
ing his great work. I intend to remain in
protest until the Lorraine is used as a
facility to help the poor and needy and
hungry.

BRAD: This is my first day in Memphis. I
came in last night and I'm leaving today,
but I see a lot of other empty buildings
around here that could be used as shelters
or whatever. Why haven't you taken any
steps to transform those buildings into
that kind of facility?

JACQUELINE: Well, this area is being gentrified and they are not going to put a homeless shelter here. In my opinion, it simply
won't be. This area has been targeted for
upgrading and the poor people will simply
be priced out. They're taking the land and
they're not making provisions for the people being displaced.

BRAD: But I heard that the motel would

have been torn down. So would you rather have just a level piece of dirt right here, or would you rather have a museum that's teaching the history of our people? Like my friends here . . . they came in and they learned a piece of my history. If this museum wasn't here they wouldn't have had the opportunity. So, in a way, it is feeding the hungry. It just fed their hungry minds and also mine.

JACQUELINE: Well, to answer your first question, I don't think the Lorraine would have been torn down. If it were placed on the National Registry of Historic Places, that would have protected it from being destroyed. As it is, half of it has been torn down. They've made it into a luxurious, hi-tech tourist-trap. That's all it is . . . cars that Dr. King never saw, this fancy wall that he never looked at . . . I don't believe for one minute that the motel was going to be demolished. That was an excuse to turn it into this. Secondly, anyone who has a serious want for knowledge concerning the civil-rights struggle has many places they can get the knowledge from. The public library is crawling with information. Let me suggest to you that you read Dr. King's books. He wrote five books. I believe if you read Dr. King's books, you'll get more about Dr. King and his philosophy than you will in the museum.

BRAD: I'm sure you will.

EILEEN: This is three-dimensional, though. You get a real feel for what went on. I think it's very educational.

JACQUELINE: Well, Dr. King certainly understood the importance of an education, but he also understood that there was some-

thing more important—the ability to feed
oneself, clothe oneself, and house oneself.
So there are first things first. What good
does that museum do for someone who's homeless or hungry? I believe that if there is a
need for this museum, it should be somewhere else. I think the Lorraine Motel
should be a commemorization of Dr. King,
rather than being shared by an institution
like the museum. It's sacred ground.

BRAD: I agree with you. Dr. King did a lot
for the civil-rights movement and for Americans in general. But he did not fight the
civil-rights battle by himself. There's a
lot of other people who died and got beat up
and lost their families. I think they did
the right thing by sharing the site with
all the people who fought for the civil-
rights movement, or at least as many as
they could. They have a special room in
there dedicated to him.

WADE: Have you ever been inside?

JACQUELINE: I worked at the Lorraine for a
number of years.

BRAD: You're not answering the question.
Have you been inside?

JACQUELINE: I watched them build it.

WADE: So you haven't been inside.

JACQUELINE: No.

BRAD: Come on, let's go inside.

JACQUELINE: I was the last person thrown
out of the hotel before it was turned into
the museum. That represents ten million
dollars in tax money. What could have been
done with that money? What they have in
there does not impress me. That's not something Dr. King would support.

A passing local gets in on the discussion.

LOCAL: That is the most courageous sister ever, man. Anybody who stays outdoors like she does . . . I'm talking every night out here on the street . . . she's braver than anybody over there. You can build all the trash and monuments you want, but that's the bravest sister out here. You come out here and sleep with her four or five nights, then you can talk that stuff. (*Raising his voice*) That woman has stayed out here thousands of days and I come by every night with prostitutes, drug dealers, everybody coming by here. I don't know what you're talking about, brother.

BRAD: Hey, I'm coming here trying to find out what she's talking about. Do you know why she's out here?

LOCAL: I was out here when he got shot. I know my history.

BRAD: But do you know why she's sitting out here?

LOCAL: Ask her. She'll tell you. She's been doing it for five years.

BRAD: I'm asking you. You're trying to straighten me out, why don't you answer my question?

LOCAL: You gotta pay your dues, brother. Have you paid yours?

The irate local storms off.

JACQUELINE: See, you're going to get that. Memphis is Memphis. We know the surroundings. We saw what happened when this went up. People lost their jobs, homes were destroyed . . . this whole area is being gentrified. Land is being taken away from

poor people. We don't have any respect for
this museum. The bottom line is that if you
want to have a serious knowledge of Dr.
King's philosophies and principles, you'll
have to crack the books.

                                    CUT TO:

INTERIOR NEON—AFTERNOON

After pondering their experience at the
museum over lunch at B. B. King's Blues
Club on Beale Street, the gang sets out for
Bolivar, Tennessee, and a taste of down-
home fun at a demolition derby.

WADE: One thing I think about this "Generation X" and all that stuff is that it seems
we're making too much of a deal about the
black/white issue and not making it everybody's issue. I mean, look at Eileen.
Nobody so far has brought up one thing
about the fact that she's minority and what
that means.

BRAD: But for the most part, Asians are
treated like Caucasians.

EILEEN: That's not true. During World War
II, they put Japanese Americans in camps
and a lot of Chinese were put there too,
just because they looked alike. Just
recently in Boston, a radio station spon-
sored this event where they bought all
these Sony products and ran them over with
a steam roller. That was their stand
against Japan.

WADE: I'm just saying if things are going to change, it can't be black, white, Asian . . .

BRAD: It should work that way and you saying that is good. But most Caucasians don't think that way.

WADE: Neither do most blacks. Just like what your dad made you do with the poster.

BRAD: But it's self-preservation. It's like Cheri says. She doesn't care enough about my African-American history or Asian history to pick up a damn book.

CHERI: No, no, no. I'm not going to pick up a white history book this year either.

BRAD: You learned white history in school.

CHERI: What did I tell you I took in school? The History of South Africa, as an elective. What I'm saying is that I'm not going to pick up a history book at all this year, and the museum was a place I could get a well-rounded overview in a short amount of time.

BRAD: You have to teach yourself, though. All my friends took the time to learn a lot about African Americans because they grew up with me. When you're in high school, all the history is white history.

CHERI: They're changing that.

BRAD: But I learned only white history. Boston Tea Party had nothing to do with my history, but I had to learn it.

EILEEN: But it's not necessarily "white" history, Brad. It's American history and you're an American.

BRAD: Then you're blind if you think that, being a minority.

CHERI: I'll tell you this: With your upbringing, you do have a skewed view. Just your dad telling you to take down the poster of a white guy puts a chip on your shoulder so that you're not trying to blend in.

BRAD: Blend in? Are you for real?

CHERI: You're not trying for unity. You're trying to stay separate.

BRAD: I wasn't taught to stay separate.

CHERI: Support your own people? If I did that . . .

BRAD: You do it every day!

CHERI: If I bought a Janet Jackson album, do you think my mom would ever say, "What are you listening to this black music for?" My brother plays in a reggae band. That's not "my" music. You're not aiding unity.

BRAD: That's totally off the point. All my friends that you saw at my house are Caucasian, but still I'm not aiding?

CHERI: I think that has a lot to do with your class there.

BRAD: You think I hang with them just because they're in my class? I live in Atlanta now. That's almost all black. You don't think I could find new black friends there? Real quick!

CHERI: It's strange you're not friends with your neighbors.

BRAD: I'm friends with some of my neighbors, but they weren't there because they're off at college. I'm not friends with losers of any kind of color.

There is a long silence in the car.

We all painted my car and it turned into a spray paint fight. I got Wade in the face. At times like these it's hard not to flirt with Wade, but we want to keep our relationship off the show. This is becoming increasingly difficult to deal with. When we are not on camera, he acts flirtatious and in pursuit. Around the crew, he goes out of his way to act indifferent. I know we agreed on this, but it's adding undue stress...

Cheri puts the finishing touches on her entry into the demolition derby. TIFFANY HOSS

It's adult bumper cars! It's fun to ram someone at top speed, outmaneuver oncoming drivers, and keep going as your car is slowly pummeled. Words can't describe it.

WADE: I think what makes the issue is that your parents and your grandparents were subject to a lot of the things in that museum. For you and us, it hasn't really been that harsh. You haven't really seen what they've seen. But they teach you what they've seen, so you're sensitive to those issues. When something comes up, it's not offending you, it's offending what you've been taught. As long as that keeps going on, it will be perpetuated.

CHERI: When I was in Europe, we met some English guys and they were going off like, "Your grandparents killed our grandparents." Come into the twentieth century. What are you talking about?

WADE: I was never taught any racial things. My mom was going out with a black guy back in like, 1976, and I could tell that people were looking at them differently, but I never had that difference ingrained in me, so I couldn't really understand it.

BRAD: A lot of things that people don't think about as racial comments are racial comments.

EILEEN: I usually say "African American." Do you prefer that or "black"?

BRAD: It doesn't matter. Racist comments to me are like if you were to say, "Denzel Washington is a good-looking black man." That, to me, is a racist comment. Why can't he be a good-looking man? That's the most offensive thing. All my friends are good-looking guys. And through high school they were considered good-looking, but then Brad was the good-looking black guy. Why couldn't I be put in the same category as my friends?

CHERI: See, I was never raised around black people, just because of where I grew up. It's all white. So something like that . . . I might have said that before.

BRAD: But that's a racist comment.

CHERI: And now that you say it, it is kind of rude. I just wouldn't have thought of it that way before.

BRAD: I know you wouldn't. That's the way it is.

They drive in silence toward Bolivar.

FADE OUT.

Wade warms up the "Miseratti" while he waits for his heat in the demolition derby.
EILEEN CHUNG

DAY 8:

TRAVEL: 347 miles/7 hours raw drive time

PLACES OF INTEREST:
Mississippi:
- Clarksdale, a major blues town in Mississippi, is home to **Wade Walton's Barbershop,** where you can get a haircut while Wade sings you the blues. 317 Issaquena Avenue. (601)6274-6067.
- **The Delta Blues Museum** showcases the roots of Delta blues from past to present and sells records, books, and souvenirs. It's located on the top floor of the Clarksdale Library. 114 Delta Avenue. (601) 624-4461.
- Turn right off Highway 61 onto Route 82 toward Greenville, Mississippi, to visit Jim Henson's boyhood home and the **Muppet Museum.**

→ **REVEREND WILLIE MORGANFIELD'S GOSPEL.** The Right Reverend starts Sunday with a singin', sweatin', soulful gospel service. The Bellgrove Church at 831 Garfield Street, Clarksdale.

PLACES TO EAT:
- **Fair's,** at 227 4th Street in Clarksdale, serves up soul food Delta-style. (601) 627-2747.

NIGHTLIFE:
New Orleans:
- **Bourbon Street** in the French Quarter has bars and music aplenty. Check out **Lafitte's Blacksmith Shop, Oz,** and the **Bourbon Pub.**
- **Cafe Istanbul** and **Cafe Brasil** churn out salsa and Latin rock in Faubourg Marigny at the corner of Frenchmen and Chartres. (504) 944-4180.

- **Tipitinas** is the bar/venue where most of the bigger acts play when they're in town. 501 Napolean. (504) 895-8477.
- **The Rock and Bowl/Zydeco Blues Emporium** has bowling and pool and, at night, hopping live zydeco music and dancing. 4133 South Carrollton Avenue. (504) 482-3133.

ACCOMMODATIONS:
New Orleans:
- **The Old Columns Hotel,** a seventeen-room converted St. Charles mansion. Mike, voted Best Bartender several years in a row, pours nightly in the bar downstairs. 3811 St. Charles. (504) 899-9308.
- **The Marquette House Youth Hostel** at 2253 Cardondelet Street. (504) 523-3014.
- **The Hotel Villa Convento** is an affordable stay in the French Quarter. 616 Ursulines Street. (504) 524-1793.

FADE IN:
INTERIOR NEON—DAY

On waking, our trippers put on their Sunday-go-to-meetin' clothes and head to the Southern Baptist Church of Reverend Willie Morganfield to check out a real revival meeting, complete with singing, sweating, and conniptions of the Holy Spirit.

Leaving the church, they pile into the Neon and head south through the cotton fields of Mississippi for New Orleans.

WADE: Man, that was intense. That guy can sing. I've never seen anything like it.

EILEEN: When I go to church, it's totally boring. You just memorize prayers and all.

BRAD: Yeah, there's nothing like a Sunday meeting to get your blood going.

CHERI: Do you think those women were

Up early, somewhat hung ... Southern Baptist Revival in Clarksdale, MO. Amazing choir, preacher (Rev. Morganfield, cousin of Muddy Waters, someone said) sang his sermon—more like a monologue—people gyrating in the audience, even had special people in white gowns that would fan the screaming parishioners.

really getting the Holy Spirit? That was nuts.

WADE: They were getting something in there.

EILEEN: It's really contagious.

WADE: It's more like a stage show.

CHERI: Live, from Clarksdale, Mississippi!

EILEEN: I haven't been to church in a while.

CHERI: I don't really go to church much. I guess I've kind of slipped away from it. I know that once I get my life together more, I'll get back into religion. Some of the things I do . . . in waitressing . . . sometimes someone will give me a fifty-dollar bill by accident and I could get away with it, but I think, "What goes around comes around." If I keep that, it's gonna have a negative effect on my life. Whether it's God watching or bad karma, or whatever, I go by those laws.

BRAD: I'm a very religious person. Sometimes I don't do everything that I should do or lead my life the way God wants me to lead it, but as far as praying to God and knowing that there is a God and one day that I want to meet Him, that there is a heaven and a hell, I was brought up Southern Baptist.

EILEEN: How do you know it's a him?

BRAD: I just use the word "Him." I don't think God is of any sex. He's just a spirit.

WADE: When it comes to religion, I have a hard time believing that there's this being called God. Or that there's a place that you go when you're done called heaven or hell. I can't believe that. People need something to believe in, that there's something more than this. I believe in "What goes around comes around." I just have trouble believing that there's a God that came down and said, "Here's this and here's this, this is made and that's made." I think that if there was someone up there, they wouldn't let happen some of the things that happen in this world.

CHERI: Religion's a difficult issue, especially being raised Catholic. The Catholic Church is so set in its ways that a lot of the rules are outdated. I've broken away and sort of formed my own beliefs around what I was originally taught. But I had priests as teachers who did that, too. They used to say that if you committed suicide, it was a mortal sin and you were going to hell. But I had a teacher who didn't see it that way. He said, "If you are in such a state of confusion that you would take your own life, you're not in your right mind. How can God condemn you to hell for that?"

WADE: I don't think God says anything like that. In every religion, they argue which one is right. I don't think that a God would come down and say, "Okay, yours is right and yours is wrong." Everybody would be the same. And I've also seen so many hypocritical people go to church, it's not even funny.

CHERI: I don't go to church right now because I don't feel like going. Maybe it's laziness, but I don't feel like going there and putting up a front and not really paying attention.

WADE: I think it just comes down to being a

The Neon takes the fast lane on the way through Mississippi. SAM JONES

good person. So many people will go to church and right after church will be an asshole about something.

BRAD: I agree with you that there's no wrong or right religion, but there is a higher being. There is a heaven and hell. In order to get through to heaven, my personal belief is that you have to be more than a good person. I believe you have to give your life to Jesus Christ and live your life for Jesus Christ.

WADE: How are you living for Jesus?

BRAD: You don't live for anything in this world. God and Jesus are not of this world and anything of this world is not godly. That means you do your best not to sin. In other words, doing things like having premarital sex—before you're married under the eyes of Jesus Christ, and knowing that it's wrong but saying, "It's okay, I'm a good person"—that's not living your life for Jesus Christ.

WADE: Okay, how would you change your life now to live for Jesus?

BRAD: Well, first you would get down on your knees. You would get down on your knees and pray. You would pray to Jesus to wipe clean all of your sins. Then you would say, "I believe in you, I believe in God, and I want to serve you in the best way I can." If you can sincerely get down on your knees and say this prayer and really mean it and change your ways . . .

WADE: But that's what I mean, how do you change your ways? What, specifically, do you do?

BRAD: That's what I'm saying. You live for Him.

WADE: By doing WHAT?

BRAD: Not having premarital sex, cursing, anything you think is wrong. Then you start helping people and spreading His word.

WADE: You're describing to me exactly what I was saying about being a good person. You're saying, "Don't cuss, don't have pre-marital sex . . ."

BRAD: And spreading His word. You can do things and say things. Like, this bartender where I work lost his father and he was feeling real down about it and he asked me for advice and I told him: "What you need to do is pray. You need to pray to God and you'll find comfort in God." Something as small as that.

CHERI: I'm more on Wade's wavelength. I think if I died today, I wouldn't be kept out of heaven because I had premarital sex. It's the little things like mowing the old lady's lawn next door that show being Christ-like. Those are all the things that get you there.

                                        CUT TO:

INTERIOR NEON—AFTERNOON

Heading south on Route 49, they make the tiny town of Greenwood for lunch.

Eileen takes the wheel as they head for New Orleans.

EILEEN: I can't wait till we get to New Orleans. Are we going to go to the House of Voodoo?

CHERI: I feel sick, like nauseous.

WADE: You don't believe in that, do you?

BRAD: Here we go again. I'm not saying anything.

CHERI: I'm going to ask the palm reader if I've got barfing in my cards.

WADE: Yeah, "By the way, am I going to yack today?"

EILEEN: You'll yack at five P.M.

WADE: Don't blow it for me. I'm gonna lie about my name. I'm going to lie about everything. If they're any good they'll know I'm lying. I'm going to say my name is Lauden Swain and I'm . . .

EILEEN: What are you going to say your name is?

WADE: That's a name I like . . . Lauden Swain.

CHERI: Where'd you get that?

WADE: It's just a name I like. If I have a boy, that's what I'm gonna name him.

CHERI: Lauden? You're going to name your son Lauden?

WADE: You haven't heard weirder names?

CHERI: Lauden. That's just lovely.

WADE: I don't care what you think. Bruce Willis named their kids Rumor and Scout. There's a couple of winners, huh?

CHERI: Lauden. That's one of the worst I've ever heard.

WADE: Or Devon. I like Devon, too.

EILEEN: I like Devon.

WADE: I don't want his name to be like, Scott.

CHERI: Lauden . . .

On the way to New Orleans, took Highway 61 through poor Southern towns. Poverty was rampant. We would see houses that appeared to be totally boarded up and then a child would come out of one. People actually live in those dilapidated shacks.

We stopped at Doe's, a restaurant listed in the guide book. When we arrived, Wade refused to eat there because it was not in the best section of town and somewhat rundown. Brad joined him. He often followed Wade's lead. Big deal—I don't know what they were being such wimps about.

EILEEN: I like the name Tyler.

BRAD: Sounds gay. He'd be a little mama's boy.

EILEEN: You're so homophobic.

BRAD: I'd take him away from his mama, slap him around some. "Come here, boy, I'm gonna make a man of you."

EILEEN: So he can be just as insensitive as you?

BRAD: I'm insensitive. I know what y'all think.

EILEEN: Well, isn't sensitivity feminine? And you don't want any part of femininity in you.

BRAD: I don't.

EILEEN: So there you go. You should be proud that you're insensitive. It's a manly quality.

BRAD: You can insult me all you want . . .

Brad was supposed to get his hair cut, but we didn't have time and we wanted to get to New Orleans. He made such a fuss. It's times like these that you can tell he is an only child.

EILEEN: I didn't say it as an insult. Sensitivity you said was feminine and you don't want to be feminine at all. You said you're one hundred percent male.

BRAD: That's right.

EILEEN: You're all set, then. You should be so excited that you're one hundred percent male. And it's not an insult.

None of us could even tell that his hair looked too long (still, it is less than a centimeter long when a strand is pulled straight).

BRAD: Do you think I'm insensitive, Wade?

EILEEN: You're so hung up.

BRAD: I'm not talking to you! You think I'm insensitive, Wade?

WADE: You want me to be perfectly honest, now?

BRAD: We talk more. You know me better than they do.

WADE: Well, you're afraid to admit your sensitivities.

BRAD: So you think I am sensitive.

WADE: You are, but you're afraid to admit it. You don't want anybody to know you are.

BRAD: You've come to this conclusion after our conversations and stuff?

WADE: Just talking to you and being around you. You're afraid to admit that you're sensitive or that you might have any weaknesses.

BRAD: That's honest. I like that you can say that without it being an insult. Unlike some people who I've been nice to this whole trip.

EILEEN: BRAD! It's not an insult! What do you think? Why don't you tell me how you think you are?

BRAD: It doesn't matter. It's obvious that you don't like me.

EILEEN: Oh, my god! I make one comment and I don't like you? Now you're being insecure.

WADE: Perfect!

CHERI: What?

FADE OUT.

As we anticipated, we arrived after 11:30 P.M. at our motel. I'm pissed! No nightlife for us in New Orleans. I'm mostly disappointed. My patience is wearing thin with the cast and crew ... the long days, the long delays, the little sleep, the little eats ... it's taking a toll on all of us!!!

DAY 9:

TRAVEL: 199 miles/4 hours raw drive time

PLACES OF INTEREST
New Orleans:
- **The French Quarter** is the old standby. Plenty of eats, drinks and local color.
- **Faubourg Marigny** is the alternative hangout in New Orleans, located at the corner of Frenchmen and Chartres.
- **The riverfront warehouse district** is where you'll find the more upscale youth culture, art galleries, cool restaurants, etc.
- Relive the acid-trip sequence in *Easy Rider* amid the above-ground tombs of the city's historic cemeteries (St. Louis No. 1 and No. 2, especially). No. 1 is at 400 Basin Street and No. 2 is at the corner of North Claiborne and Bienville.
- One of the most popular pastimes in the Big Easy is **tubing.** Grab a forty-piece bucket of chicken from Popeye's, a case of your favorite beverage and an inner tube, and float down one of the many tributaries of the Mississippi. One of the best starting points is Black Creek, Mississippi.
- Uptown is the home of **Loyola** and **Tulane** universities and a hub of the college crowd.
- Have your palms read at **Marie Laveau's House of Voodoo,** 739 Bourbon Street. (504) 581-3751.
- **Hot Wax** record store at 722 Orleans Street is the place to stop in and browse for everything from Abba to Zydeco.

PLACES TO EAT:
- **Eddie's,** a hole-in-the-wall that locals claim has some of the best Creole food in the city. 2119 Law Street. (504) 945-2207.
- **The Camellia Grill,** located uptown, has great

The four of us cruised Bourbon Street. Strange bars, shops, naked women, naked men, sex toy stores—anything and everything. Eileen and I dressed up like bar sluts and the guys like cowboys to get a daguerreotype photograph.

breakfast fare. 626 South Carrollton Avenue.
(504) 866-9573.

- **Cafe Istanbul and Cafe Brasil** in Faubourg Marigny
are restaurants that also have live performances at
night. 534 Frenchmen Street. (504) 944-4180.

- **Mandina's** on Canal Street in the mid-city section
is an upscale restaurant where you might spot Harry
Connick, Jr., or Branford Marsalis if they're in
town. 3800 Canal Street. (504) 482-9179.

- **Johnny's Po-Boys** at 511 St. Louis Street. Don't
leave the city without trying one of their Po-Boy
sandwiches. (504) 524-8129.

ACCOMMODATIONS:
- **Motel 6,** 546 MacArthur Drive, Alexandria,
Louisiana. (318) 445-2336.

FADE IN:
EXTERIOR NEW ORLEANS—DAY

Having spent the night in a motel just outside the city, the cast drives into New
Orleans and finds the French Quarter.

Brad and Wade spend the day walking around
the city looking for a barber shop where
Brad can get his hair cut. Eileen and Cheri
cruise the Cajun Market and shops along
Bourbon Street.

Finally finding a barber shop, Wade leaves
Brad to get his trim and meets back up with
the girls just as they are about to get
their palms read.

CHERI: I can't believe you guys spent all
day looking for a barber shop.

WADE: Brad's still sitting there.

CHERI: Waiting to get his hair cut?

WADE: Yeah. The barber shop was filled.

EILEEN: Was it like he said?

WADE: Right out of the movie. All these guys are just going on and on, arguing about this and that . . . barely making sense most of the time. It was a riot.

CHERI: I'm going to get my palm read.

She approaches one of the many palmists that line the waterfront of the French Quarter. Jerik, the palmist, is a large gentle man with long blond hair and a quick smile.

CHERI: Hey, how you doing?

JERIK: Well, surviving another fun-filled afternoon. Are you interested in a piece of palmistry today?

CHERI: Yeah.

JERIK: Well, have a seat by all means.

CHERI: Thanks.

JERIK: My pleasure. My name is Jerik. I've been here for twenty-one years, so you've come to one of the old pros. I will explain what I'm doing as we go along, so you'll learn something about palmistry when we're done. Give me your right hand. There are about twelve different types of palms as far as shapes. You have the craftperson's hands. The widely spaced fingers indicate being broad-minded and versatile, able to do more than one thing. You're the one who says, "Hi, I can do my job and the person's to the left or right of me." What we have here is your life line. Yours is a long one. I hope you enjoy living. You're going to be around to do so for a great many years. You have what we call a deeply etched life line which indicates a strong vitality. You're

Cheri sports a Mardi Gras mask while shopping in the French Market in New Orleans. EILEEN CHUNG

Our meal at the Court of Two Sisters was $200 for the four of us. Not to sound unappreciative, but I would have rather taken my $50 and spent a fraction of it eating at a hole-in-the-wall Creole restaurant. The food would have been just as good and there'd probably have been larger portions.

the kind who, whether you drink or smoke or tell naughty jokes, your vitality is going to be very high. You have what we call tension lines at the beginning of your life line. That shows that you've had at least one pain-in-the-ass relative and some challenging situations along your way. Your mound of Mars tells me that you're ninety percent niceness and ten percent tigress by the tail. Some people only see the nice part and forget that the tigress is in there, but they are reminded from time to time. The tigress in your case will be revealed as scathing sarcasm. Your mound of Luna is very high, indicating that you're a daydreamer. You're a space cadet. Your mound of Mercury makes you a born communicator. You can talk to anyone about anything. That's the kind of person who can basically sell refrigerators to Eskimos and leave them liking it. You have a broad gap between your Mercury and Apollo fingers. That indicates that for you, money is a liquid resource. You get it and you help it go away again. Your mound of Apollo says you're just at the start of your creativity in life. This again will play into your communication skills. You have a low mound of Saturn, which is hysterical, and I'll tell you why. A low mound of Saturn is a little girl masquerading as a grown-up. Inside you're still a twelve-year-old brat. Your mound of Jupiter indicates indulgence. If some is good, some more is better. You will be a financial success. You have an energy level like the Energizer bunny. You have an excellent line of heart. It has some breaks in it. That means that you've kissed your share of frogs trying to find your prince. With this line of heart, however, is longtime friendships. You're very psychic. When I say that, I don't mean in a trained or formal way. You will have strong feelings about things that you will follow to great success. You have a wonderful palm and it's been my pleasure to interpret it.

WADE: That was pretty good.

JERIK: Thank you. I've been a reader for twenty-one years. It's a learnable skill. I don't think of it as magic. The life of everyone is interpretable and it's just a matter of memorization, really. It's not as occult as everyone thinks. It's just a skill that can be learned by anyone with patience and intelligence.

Brad arrives, his hair freshly cropped.

BRAD: Okay, okay . . . let's get a move on! Dinner's waiting for us.

They climb into the Neon and drive to The Court of Two Sisters for dinner.

                              CUT TO:

INTERIOR NEON—DUSK

As the sun sets, the cast rolls off toward Alexandria, Louisiana, putting some miles behind them for the long drive to Dallas.

EILEEN: I hate to leave. New Orleans is so beautiful.

WADE: That food isn't half bad, either.

EILEEN: What are you reading, Brad?

BRAD: This Kung Fu magazine. They're talk-ing about the old days and training for Kung Fu and stuff. One guy wanted to be trained so bad that he stood outside the master's house for weeks and finally cut off his own left arm and offered it to him to show him he was sincere about learning.

EILEEN: That's dedication.

CHERI: That's stupidity.

BRAD: This is back in the eighteenth century, though. Everything was more violent back then.

WADE: You don't think it's more violent today?

CHERI: Now it is. People used to leave their doors unlocked and let their children roam the neighborhood . . .

WADE: I remember when I grew up I just ran wherever I wanted to go and didn't worry about it.

CHERI: Now parents will drive their kids even a few blocks to school because they're worried that their kid'll be taken away.

WADE: Look at your father's prison. He said they get like five new people in there every week. That's a lot of people over the course of a year.

EILEEN: And look at things like cartoons today.

WADE: Yeah. I used to watch Bugs Bunny. Everything today is just kill 'em, kill 'em, kill 'em.

EILEEN: That's where it starts, on television.

CHERI: It's also drugs. I mean, there used to be drugs like acid and things like that. They were more nonviolent. Crack just makes people nuts.

EILEEN: And guns.

WADE: I don't think it's guns. It's people. I don't see why someone shouldn't own a gun. I mean, the gun's not jumping into your hand and controlling you.

CHERI: When you have a gun in your house, Wade, a lot of times it gets used against someone you know. Accidental deaths, like when kids get ahold of them. That kind of goes against what you're saying.

WADE: But it's called handling your gun safely. Drugs are a much bigger problem than guns. I mean, I've heard things where some countries count drug sales as part of the income of the state. That's crazy.

BRAD: But it's all tied together. They swap guns for drugs. People who work for the DEA and certain circles of the CIA have documented the fact that the government will send guns to South American guerrillas and countries down there in exchange for letting drugs into this country. So you got the same law enforcement agents fighting against drugs that are helping to bring them in.

EILEEN: I don't believe that, entirely. I think there's corruption, but I don't think it's built into the system like that.

CHERI: What if they just made drugs legal? That way you could really control them and really make money on taxes like they do on alcohol.

BRAD: I think marijuana should be legalized.

EILEEN: You do?

BRAD: Yeah, but marijuana is not part of the problem. Not at all. Cigarettes and drinking will hurt you just as bad as marijuana. I haven't heard of too many people who are selling their bodies for marijuana or robbing somebody or killing somebody or breaking into somebody's house to buy marijuana. I would tax it and use all the taxes that came off the sale of marijuana and put it toward education and rehab for other drugs.

EILEEN: You'd just be encouraging people to do something bad for them.

WADE: There's other things just as bad. Alcohol is just as bad.

BRAD: I did a paper on this. They said that marijuana is no worse for you than alcohol. It kills just as many brain cells.

CHERI: And if you taxed it, think of all the good that money could do. You could pay for AIDS research or cancer research.

EILEEN: What about kids that get ahold of it?

WADE: Well you'd have to be twenty-one, just like alcohol.

EILEEN: But kids get ahold of alcohol anyway.

WADE: Kids get ahold of pot anyway. We need regular education for younger people. In Oregon, they've cut billions of dollars from education. They cut schools so bad. What are you supposed to do?

BRAD: What Cheri was saying earlier is right. Most of the murderers that you were talking about had been in trouble when they were younger. And if somebody had caught them when they were young, they wouldn't have committed the crime.

EILEEN: I agree with Wade, though. We

should spend the money on kids who aren't in trouble and want to learn.

CHERI: You don't have to take money from education. Say you're going to build a prison. You take that money and instead of building a regular prison, you make it into one of these boot camps.

EILEEN: Are they the same in cost?

BRAD: A boot camp would be a lot cheaper.

CHERI: I think the problem is men, too. They're more violent. I see it in Brad. When he gets upset about something he turns his sorrow or whatever and turns it into anger. I'm just the opposite. If I get mad I get frustrated and turn it into emotion and just . . .

WADE: Bawl. Right?

CHERI: Yeah, I bawl. You guys use your emotions differently.

BRAD: When a little boy is walking around and he falls down and scrapes his knee, his dad or his mom will say, "Shhh. Don't cry. Be a tough little man." But when a little girl falls and starts crying it's like, "There, there, it'll be all right, go ahead and cry, let it out."

WADE: The man has to be strong. He has to be the breadwinner.

BRAD: Yeah. That too. That's why you have more male drug dealers than you do female drug dealers. When a boy goes to high school, he sees all them pretty girls and he might be from a ghetto or a poor family, and he wants to meet these girls and date these girls. Instead of working at McDonald's, he's going to deal drugs to the point where he can afford nice clothes and a nice car.

CHERI: There's also a lot more peer pressure among guys. Guys are always razzing each other, daring each other to do things.

WADE: It's not a perfect society. We're not perfect people. It's just not that way. If it was, everyone would be raising perfect kids and nobody would be committing crimes and none of this stuff would be happening. Most likely you raise your kids the same way you were raised yourself.

BRAD: Wade's a pretty masculine guy, but still he's Mr. Sensitive and cries at movies and all that. He can express himself, that's fine. There's a happy medium. But I'm happy the way I am, and I'm going to raise my kid the same way.

EILEEN: What if you have girls?

BRAD: I'm not planning on having girls.

EILEEN: How can you plan on having one or the other?

BRAD: Well, at this point, I don't know how I would do it. Hopefully I would have a wife and she could help me and guide me through it.

WADE: It's different with girls. You have to be careful with them because they're the ones who get pregnant. The guy doesn't.

CHERI: You might have to treat girls differently in that way, but I also think there shouldn't be this thing where Dad's like, "Good boy, way to go." If a guy goes and sleeps around, he's a stud. If a girl does it, she's a slut. I'm going to tell my daughter, "Look, this is what happens. This is the kind of reputation you can get." It should all be laid on the line.

BRAD: I'll tell you, it's kind of hard

being a male when your son comes home like that. You may not want to, but you're gonna crack a smile because you remember when you were that age. You'll remember your first kiss or whatever. You're gonna be smiling inside.

CHERI: I think you can be excited about that, but at the same time you have to say, "Yeah, you are taking a step into manhood, but part of being a man is learning to respect women. So you shouldn't go around bragging to people about it."

BRAD: I think most fathers do that, though. I think you're saying that just because a father pats his son on the back means that he's saying, "Go out and disrespect women." My father patted me on the back, but he still taught me to respect women. I think you can do both. If a girl lets a guy go so far, and the guy goes so far, he hasn't disrespected her. As long as he doesn't force anything on her, he's not disrespecting. If she feels bad about it later, then she's disrespected herself.

CHERI: It's all about respect. I'm not saying that girls are all victims, but a lot of times a girl's first time will be because she thinks she's in love and the guy has a different agenda.

EILEEN: The stud mentality is definitely going out, though. It left with John Travolta and *Saturday Night Fever.*

BRAD: It may be changing, but it's not that dramatic.

FADE OUT.

DAY 10:

TRAVEL: 311 miles/6.2 hours raw drive time

PLACES OF INTEREST:
- If you're in the market for authentic western wear, stop off at **Cooper's Cowboy Store** on I-84 on your way out of Mansfield, Louisiana. It's been in the Cooper family since 1946, when it started as a general store. Say hello to Rocky, the pet boxer, who roams the floors.
- Feeling morbid? Check out **Jerry's Market and Taxidermy Shop** at the intersection of I-84 and Route 59 in Marshall, Texas.
- Hit Dallas early to visit **Deep Ellum,** the hippest district in Dallas. You'll find restaurants, clubs, galleries, and theaters.

PLACES TO EAT:
Dallas:
- **Aw, Shucks** at 3601 Greenville Avenue has cheap, good seafood. Highly recommended. (214) 821-9449.
- **Deep Ellum Cafe** at 2706 Elm Street was the first restaurant in the area. (214) 741-9012.
- **Tolbert's** at 1800 North Market Street has X-rated chili. Taste it for yourself. (214) 969-0310.

NIGHTLIFE:
- **Cafe Dada** at 2720 Elm Street in Deep Ellum was the birthplace of Edie Brickell and New Bohemians. (214) 744-DADA.
- **Cowboys** is a huge honky-tonk. Try your feet at the two-step. (214) 321-0115.
- **Billy Bob's** in Fort Worth is a restaurant with the last remaining mechanical bull. 2520 Rodeo Plaza. (817) 589-1711.
- **Fishdance** is an unlikely *Saturday Night Fever-*

meets-*Moby-Dick* venue. 3606 Greenville Avenue.
(214) 828-2277.

ACCOMMODATIONS:
- **Motel 6,** 4325 Beltline Road, Dallas.
(214) 386-4579.

FADE IN:
INTERIOR NEON—DAY

Wanting to get a jump on the day, the cast
sets out early for Dallas.

WADE: You ever watch "Beavis and Butt-
Head"?

CHERI: Yeah. Hilarious.

WADE: They kill me. How about the female
mud wrestling one where they were going to
go to the mud wrestling thing . . .

EILEEN: Did you ever see the "Sick and
Twisted Festival"? It's got Ren and Stimpy
in it, too.

WADE: I don't like them so much.

EILEEN: So, Cheri, have you been looking
for a job?

CHERI: Thinking about it. Thinking about
looking.

EILEEN: Do you know what you want to do?
That seems like the hardest part.

CHERI: Yeah, well, what I have to do is
check out some more mortgage companies. I
might do that, or I might not even go in
that direction. I might do something with
travel. Then I would get to travel. I don't
really have a set goal. I wouldn't mind
working for a large corporation in fore-

casting and budgeting or something . . . use my mind a little bit. That's what I didn't like about my last job. I didn't have to think enough.

EILEEN: What did you do in your last job?

CHERI: I worked for a financial services company. I set up employee benefits pack-ages, health packages, things like that. The division I was working for went under, so I don't know what I'm going to do. I might just move somewhere for a while. I don't really have any ties now.

EILEEN: Are your friends working? Are they in school or what?

CHERI: My best friend, Lisa, is a physical therapist. My girlfriend, Rebecca, who's my roommate's sister, is in nursing school. The girls I graduated from college with are all pretty much working.

EILEEN: Are they all still in St. Louis?

CHERI: They weren't, but now they are. One is in Florida somewhere, the one I don't really get along with. My roommate, Gina, just graduated as a radiological technician or something. She doesn't have a job yet. She just went to Arizona for a month.

EILEEN: What was she doing, just hanging out?

CHERI: Yeah, her sister lives there, so she just went and veged for a while. Then my girlfriend, Dee, she was one of my best friends, she moved to Utah.

EILEEN: She's the one who became a Mormon?

CHERI: Yeah. She got married. She has a two-year-old. She'll be moving back in December.

EILEEN: It's so weird to think of that. Girls I graduated with from high school, I know some of them who are married and have kids. I mean, it's shocking, "You're twenty. What are you thinking?"

CHERI: There were four of us who really hung around together. Karen, she moved to Texas. She eloped.

EILEEN: Did her parents not approve or something?

CHERI: No, she became real religious. She's a born-again Christian. She called me one weekend and she's like, "We're getting married next weekend down in Mexico." That's so Karen, though.

EILEEN: Did you meet the guy at all?

CHERI: No. He sent a videotape to her parents to ask for her hand. He was going to come up, but something happened . . . he couldn't get out of work or something. So they eloped. I was like, "Karen, you're going to miss out on the whole wedding thing, the presents . . ." She was like, "We just want to spend our lives together." I said, "You just can't hold off on the sex."

EILEEN: That's funny.

CHERI: She's the one who had the baby at six months and it passed away after five hours. So those are all my girlfriends. Guy friends? Most of them are still in school or kinda moseying their way through school. A couple are in grad school.

They stop in Logansport, Louisiana, for a quick lunch and continue the drive.

Wade takes the wheel.

WADE: *(to Cheri)* This is something I still can't understand: When we were in Washington, why did you get so upset that I didn't talk at lunch?

CHERI: A big part of it was that I thought you were just like, "No, we're not gonna talk and we're being stubborn." I got all freaked out.

WADE: Why?

CHERI: I explained that. Brad said he wasn't going to talk. I knew Eileen wasn't going to say much . . .

BRAD: Once I got started, I talked a lot.

WADE: The whole thing, to this day, is that I don't understand why you would be mad if we didn't talk. It has nothing to do with you.

CHERI: Well, right or wrong, I felt like everything was on my shoulders. Granted, it was self-imposed pressure . . .

WADE: That's your own fault.

CHERI: You can look at it that way. I'm just telling you how I felt.

BRAD: It was all a misunderstanding. I think Wade just didn't have anything to say. I don't think he has faith in our justice system and the way politics is done in this country.

CHERI: Is that the way you feel about it, Wade?

WADE: Yeah, I do. Look at every political campaign you've ever seen. All they do is backstab the other guy to death, find any dirt they can. It's all just a big game. They don't give a shit about it. They just want to get in office. Once they get there, they got it made. How does a bill take ten years to pass? Obviously because people are not working together. Argue about something for ten years? Something's wrong there. And did you see the phony-ass smile they had on their faces when they were talking to us? You could see it a mile away. I hate phoniness like that. What was I supposed to say to them? I vote when it comes time to vote, but I don't get involved with that political stuff. That's what it is: who's got the most money to run the best campaign, who makes the most friends.

BRAD: Who kisses the most butt.

WADE: You guys don't think it's like that?

EILEEN: I'm not sure I would be that extreme about it.

CHERI: You can make things happen. Just like in St. Louis, sure there is a lot of red tape. And it's not run in the most efficient or just way, but you can still get things done.

WADE: I didn't say that. I said they don't. Why does it take that many years to get something done?

CHERI: But what I'm saying is I don't have the attitude like, just throw in the towel and I'm not going to have anything to do with it.

WADE: I said I vote. If I threw in the towel, I wouldn't vote. I just don't have anything to say to those people because I don't think they're on the up-and-up. And I don't think the politicians from St. Louis are different from anywhere else when they have their campaigns. They look for dirt just like anywhere else. I mean, George

Clinton smoked a joint? Big deal. It's all just meaningless dirt.

BRAD: *(laughing)* He's the master of funk, ain't he?

WADE: Who?

BRAD: George Clinton. He's the master of funk.

WADE: You know what I mean. Bill. Bill Clinton.

BRAD: You made me think of "Atomic Dog" when you said that.

WADE: I mean, we're obviously better than any other country in the world, but I just don't care for all that.

BRAD: I think all of them are greedy and selfish and want to better themselves instead of bettering this country, but it's almost like you're voting for the lesser of two evils. You've got to be able to look back and say, "Okay, when this guy was state representative for Louisiana, he voted for this bill and that bill. And this guy over here from Texas, he voted for this bill and this bill." And you find out which bills he voted for will better help your family and your life-style and you vote for that candidate.

WADE: They're not voting for you, though. They're voting for themselves.

BRAD: If they would work together, a lot in this country would get done in the next six months. Like Bill Clinton's health reform plan. The Republicans are fighting that to the hilt.

EILEEN: Actually, a lot of them agree with a lot of the points. It's better than a lot of other programs.

BRAD: The Republicans are trying to push their own plan through and it's exactly the same plan except for one or two points. I read it in *USA Today*. Just because Clinton's a Democratic, they have to fight it.

EILEEN: Well, I know a lot of times Republicans and Democrats don't work together, but I heard that on this issue they are.

BRAD: But that's only because Bush came in and backed Clinton on his plan.

WADE: I mean, do you think they're going to listen to what you guys say, and when you leave the room, they jot it all down and say, "Okay, we've got to work on this and this"? Right.

CHERI: I'm not saying that we're going to change anything right there, but . . .

WADE: I'm saying that we're not even a Cliff Note in their big scheme. I think they sat down for publicity.

> Wade and I got in a major fight … maybe we should just be friends. Although I didn't like that idea, I knew it was probably best…

CUT TO:

EXTERIOR ROADSIDE—AFTERNOON

Cheri and Eileen cajole Brad and Wade into stopping the car at one of the many front yards filled with roadside junk and misplaced cultural icons.

The guys elect to stay in the car while the girls browse among the relics that litter the front yard of eighty-year-old Willie Mae McCoy.

As the girls enter the fenced-in yard, Willie Mae, a gray-haired African American, strolls out of her bright blue clapboard house.

CHERI: Hi there! We're driving across the country and we saw your yard so we thought we'd stop and take a look.

WILLIE MAE: Well, *sooo* many people have been along here and they take pictures and they'll send me a bunch of them back.

EILEEN: What made you do this with your yard?

WILLIE MAE: Well, I tell you, this man used to come by here with all kinds of things he was selling. He'd come by up there where that old barn is. I took so much from him that a lot of things he would set aside, thinkin' that I'd want 'em. Then that windmill there, I ordered that from a company. Then I ordered those two little ones.

EILEEN: Did you do this all by yourself?

WILLIE MAE: Yup, did it all by myself. That old stove over there, that was sittin' out in the next pasture, and I got my brothers to go over there and get it.

EILEEN: How long have you been doing this?

WILLIE MAE: Oh, a long while.

CHERI: You have all kinds of things on this stove. It looks like while you're working you'll have a beer or two.

WILLIE MAE: *(laughs)* I don't drink much beer, but I find them cans round and about and just put 'em out where they can be seen. That wishing well over there, I ordered that, too. I'm big on orderin' stuff. I have two brothers and I'm the only sister. We all live together. Go ahead and look around all you like.

Cheri and Eileen stroll among the mountains of broken dolls, painted soda cans, empty bird cages, discarded appliances, hubcaps, empty milk cartons, and other artifacts.

CHERI: Did your brothers help you do this?

WILLIE MAE: Nope. I did this all myself. My brother used to live across the road a piece, but he got sick and decided to come on and stay over here.

EILEEN: Can I take your picture?

WILLIE MAE: Only if you send me one back. My name is Willie Mae McCoy. Y'all be sure to send me some pictures back.

EILEEN: Sure. What's your address?

WILLIE MAE: Here, take one of these envelopes. I don't need it. I get all this mail and catalogs and books from people with my address and they don't even know me.

After taking their snapshots, the girls return to the car and roll onward toward Dallas.

FADE OUT.

We were all happy to get to Dallas. First we chowed down and then we began drinking. We're starting to get to know the crew. Wade spent most of the night whispering with Jeff (Econoboy) and disappearing with him intermittently. This was making me uncomfortable. I didn't know if he was talking about me or what. We're starting to need our space....

DAY 11:

Wednesday, October 6:

Day Off in Dallas

Went to the Beale Street Bar, which was a strange scene. We felt like the guys didn't want us there, so I spent most of my time talking to Sam and a couple of others. Wade left mad because he thought I was talking about him. Brad left with a girl. I admit, I was jealous. I don't know Wade that well. I thought I could trust him, but that was being totally naive. I tried to put it out of my mind. Hung out with Jeff till 4:00 A.M. and we talked a lot about Wade. Eileen was crashed when I got back to our room.

Take a load off.

Do your laundry.

Sit by the pool.

Contemplate your navel.

The day is yours.

DAY 12:

TRAVEL: 366 miles/7.5 hours raw drive time

PLACES OF INTEREST:
Dallas:
- **The JFK Memorial** and **Texas School Book Depository**
in Dallas. You've seen the movie, you've read the
books. Stand on the grassy knoll and decide for
yourself. 701 Calmers Street. (214) 653-0457.
- **Southfork Ranch.** The first hit nighttime soap wasn't
really shot in Dallas, but in the nearby town of
Wylie, Texas. The ranch now houses a "Dallas" museum
and gift shop. 3600 Hogge Drive. (214) 442-7897.
- Shop till you drop at *The Dallas Galleria*—
it's . . . like . . . the most incredible mall . . .
ever! L.B.J. Freeway at the Dallas Parkway.
(214) 702-7100.
- **The Reunion Tower** supports an enormous ball of
glass that houses a top-notch restaurant and
affords the best view in the city. 300 Reunion
Boulevard. (214) 651-1234.

→ **WILL ROGERS CHAMPIONSHIP RODEO,** in Tulsa—where
Wade's gonna ride a REAL, LIVE, SNORTIN', BUCKIN'
BULL. Also, chute-dogging, rescue barrel racing,
and other ropin' and wranglin' events. The rodeo is
part of the state fair, so grab yourself a corn dog
and some cotton candy and meet me at the Ferris
wheel.

PLACES TO EAT:
- **El Adobe** boasts the finest Mexican fare in the town
of Atoka, Oklahoma. In fact, it may be the only Mexican fare in Atoka. On Route 69 in the center of
town.
- They say truckers know where to get the best food.

Try the **Atoka Truck Stop** for burgers and fries. On
Route 69.

ACCOMMODATIONS:
- Motel 6, 5828 West Skelly Drive, Tulsa.
(918) 445-0223.

FADE IN:
INTERIOR NEON—MORNING

After a day off from travel and filming, the
cast departs Dallas with a new energy. Wade
steers the car toward Tulsa, Oklahoma,
where he will ride a bull at the state fair.

Cameramen Craig Spirko and Jonathan Rho
set up for one of the infamous "drive-bys"
at the Oklahoma state line. SAM JONES

CHERI: Oh, man, I'm just slap-happy today.

WADE: What does that mean, slap-happy?
Does that mean you want a slap?

CHERI: Slap-happy? I'm not really sure.

WADE: Isn't that weird the way people have
these sayings and you don't really know
what they mean? Like, "Have your cake and
eat it, too."

CHERI: Well, you know what that means. You
can't have it anymore, because you already
ate it.

WADE: Okay, "A bird in the hand is
worth . . ."

EILEEN AND CHERI: . . . two in the bush.

WADE: Two in the bush?

BRAD: What the hell does that mean?

EILEEN: It means it's better to have something than to have it out there but you
don't have it. There's another one that
goes, "A man in the house is worth two on
the street."

WADE: Don't put the cart before . . .

EILEEN: I don't know that one.

CHERI: . . . the horse.

BRAD: What does that mean? *(to Eileen)* Come on, Ms. Know-it-all.

EILEEN: I already said I don't know that one. I never said I was a know-it-all. You're the one who always says you know it all.

WADE: People in glass houses . . .

EILEEN: . . . shouldn't throw stones!

BRAD: Was that directed at me?

EILEEN: I've got one. Brad, say, "Tin," ten times.

BRAD: Tin tin tin tin tin tin tin tin tin tin.

EILEEN: What's an aluminum can made out of?

BRAD: Tin.

Everyone laughs.

BRAD: What's funny about that?

WADE: You don't get it?

EILEEN: He doesn't get it.

BRAD: An aluminum can is made out of tin.

WADE: Brad, listen to what you're saying.

BRAD: Ohhhh. That was a good one. Hahaha. That was a good one. I'll get you back for that, too.

We had lunch at a Mexican place.
Brad had never eaten Mexican food.

WADE: Okay, I've got one for you. If a bum can make a cigarette out of every four cigarette butts he finds, how many cigarettes can he make out of sixteen butts?

CHERI: Let me think. Five.

BRAD: Four.

WADE: You have to explain your answer.

CHERI: Four goes into sixteen four times. And with those four, he made one more cigarette.

BRAD: That's why you said five? That's pretty good. Okay, check this out. If a plane crashes right on the borderline between here and Canada, where do you bury the survivors?

EILEEN: You don't bury survivors.

BRAD: Man, I trick them stupid people back home with that all the time. They sit there, "Duh, Canada." Okay, I got another one. A boy and his dad . . .

EILEEN: . . . are driving in a car.

Brad stops.

EILEEN: No, go ahead and say it anyway because they might not have heard it.

BRAD: A boy and his dad are driving in a car and they have a wreck. Both of them are in bad condition. Umm . . . wait a minute . . .

EILEEN: You want me to tell it?

BRAD: Wait, I'm saying it wrong. There's names that go along with it.

EILEEN: No, the names don't matter.

BRAD: The boy's name is Bob and the dad's name is Bob Senior. The boy's name is Bob Junior. The boy's with his dad and they get in a wreck. They rush the boy to the hospital and go into the emergency room. The

Wade was as flirtatious as ever. I didn't know how to deal with mixed signals, so I blew him off (for a while). Did Oklahoma sign drive-by. The cast (mostly Wade and Brad) get really annoyed when we do those drive-bys. Eileen doesn't say much and I've pretty much accepted them as part of the trip.

doctor says, "I can't operate because this is my son, Bob." What relation is the doctor to the boy?

WADE: WHAT?

EILEEN: You're not saying it right.

BRAD: Okay, say it.

EILEEN: Okay, a boy and his father are driving and they get into a terrible accident. The father dies immediately. The boy is rushed to the hospital. The doctor walks in and looks at the table and says, "I can't operate. This is my son." How is that possible?

WADE: You said a boy and his father are in the car accident.

CHERI: The father dies immediately.

EILEEN: And the doctor says, "I can't operate because it's my son."

CHERI: The kid was adopted.

EILEEN: No.

WADE: Stepdad.

EILEEN: No.

BRAD: Don't tell them anything else. They should get it right there . . . especially Mr. Sensitive back there.

Long pause.

WADE: Man, that drives me nuts!

BRAD: I'm very disappointed in Wade, because he's supposed to be Mr. Sensitive back there. I figured it out first time I heard it just like that.

EILEEN: Oh, Brad, you're *sooo* smart.

CHERI: It was the mother! The doctor was the mother!

BRAD: See that, it never occurred to y'all that they had women doctors. Usually women get it right away.

WADE: Okay, that's enough of that.

BRAD: Hey, in that John Wayne movie, this is the river they crossed over to get to Texas. That John Wayne movie, *Red River.* He and his son had to get the cattle across the river.

Pause . . .

WADE: We should get that book of questions. There's all these questions and you can literally talk about them for hours.

EILEEN: It's a book?

WADE: It's a book with all these questions about morals and everything. We'll find out what little morals we all have.

BRAD: Y'all don't have many. Y'all are the most moral-less people I ever met in my life.

WADE: You're not old enough to have any yet.

CHERI: You don't have any morals.

BRAD: You! You got less morals than I do. I drink my milk. You're just a player. You're a bigger player than I am.

CHERI: What's that supposed to mean? Mr. Talk-to-a-woman-for-five-minutes-and-pick-them-up.

BRAD: I don't think so.

WADE: I think we just about beat that one to death.

BRAD: That's what I'm saying. Let them dead dogs lie! Let lying dogs sleep! Bury the hatchet and don't leave the handle sticking out!

EILEEN: *(laughing)* Where do you get all these sayings? You memorize books?

BRAD: Just people I'm around. They say stuff and I just pick it up.

WADE: Look at all these fences and no cattle.

BRAD: There's a cow right over there.

WADE: Okay, one. But there's miles and miles of fields.

BRAD: You don't worry about it. After you ride that bull, you won't want to see another cow the rest of your life.

WADE: Maybe you should pull over here and let me practice on that one.

A herd of cattle ponder a fire set to clear scrub from a field in Oklahoma. SAM JONES

                                    CUT TO:

INTERIOR NEON—EVENING

As the sun sets, the cast closes in on Tulsa. Brad is driving while Billy Joel sings "Honesty" on the radio. Wade and Cheri are asleep in the back and Eileen is trying to stay awake in the passenger seat.

BRAD: If I could just close my eyes for an hour I'd be all right. I just need to nap for an hour.

EILEEN: You want me to drive?

BRAD: You're already sleepy.

EILEEN: So?

BRAD: Well, I'm sleepy, but I trust myself

more than I trust you. Usually I can catch myself before I fall asleep.

Billy Joel winds up and Garth Brooks comes on the radio with "If Tomorrow Never Comes."

BRAD: YES!

EILEEN: What?

BRAD: Listen to the words of this song. I sung this song to Lauren one time. She cried when I sung this to her.

Garth breaks into the chorus:

RADIO: "If tomorrow never comes . . . will she know how much I love her?"

EILEEN: Did you ever tell her you love her?

BRAD: No. I want to, bad. I just can't.

EILEEN: Why not?

BRAD: I don't know. I just can't. I tell her I love her after we get off the phone. She doesn't ever hear it.

EILEEN: If you feel it, you should be able to say it.

BRAD: She tells me. I just can't tell her. I feel just like that song. I sung it to her when we were going together. She knows I still love her.

EILEEN: You haven't told her, so how does she know?

BRAD: She ought to be able to feel it. I swear I'd die for that girl.

EILEEN: So, when you get off the phone,

she says, "I love you," and you say, "Okay, catch you later."

BRAD: She knows how I am. She knows I'd kill for her and I'd die for her. I'd swap my soul for her. I'd go straight to hell for her. I just can't tell her.

EILEEN: You should just say it.

BRAD: It would just complicate things. She'd want to get back together. It would complicate things with her parents. Sometimes you've got to show your love by not saying anything. You know what I'm saying? She's dating a white guy now, but she doesn't love him. But he treats her good and her parents are happy. She says she still loves me, but . . . some things a man has to live with. I'd give anything in my world to forget about her. I don't even like messing with other girls. I just do it and I think about her. Then I feel guilty.

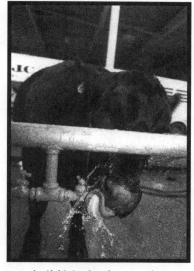

I wonder if this is what they mean by a "tongue bath." SAM JONES

Silence between them as the radio plays soft and low.

                              CUT TO:

INTERIOR NEON—NIGHT

After stopping at their motel to check in, our travelers climb back in the car and head for the rodeo.

CHERI: So, Wade, what's gonna happen with the bull? Are they going to instruct you?

WADE: Yeah. They better.

CHERI: What did your mom say about it?

WADE: She didn't want me to do it. I told her I'd call her when I was done.

CHERI: People really eat bull testicles?

While Wade prepared for his bull ride, Eileen, Brad, and I went on the amusement park rides, had gyros, and were interviewed on a huge Ferris wheel. All of us were worried that something would happen to Wade. As the bull-riding time neared, I started getting a knot in my stomach. Even the experienced bull riders often get hurt, I thought. One rider got horned in the face and it was sickening! I just wanted Wade to fall off and get out of there. Time crawled. Wade did great! As much as he drives me nuts, I still feared for him. He immediately called his mom to say that he was OK. How cute.

WADE: Yup. Delicacy.

CHERI: Wow. What are they supposed to taste like?

WADE: I don't know. I hear they taste like chicken.

BRAD: That's what everybody says about everything. Frog legs, alligator, everything's supposed to taste like chicken.

WADE: Why eat anything else, then? Why not just eat chicken? I'm hungry.

They pull into the fairgrounds.

WADE: There's a helluva lot of people here.

BRAD: You're gonna see some real damn cowboys tonight, ain't you?

WADE: This is gonna be sweet, man. There's a fair and everything. I just want to see that beast before I do anything.

BRAD: There you go, man. You'll be riding that. He ain't got no horns, though.

WADE: Oh, Jesus.

BRAD: That's probably the one they'll let you ride, 'cause it ain't got no horns.

CHERI: It just looks so massive.

WADE: They are massive. Jesus, as long as I don't have any broken bones, that'll be fine.

BRAD: Yeah. That would be my worry.

CHERI: I want to go on the roller coaster!

CUT TO:

EXTERIOR RODEO—NIGHT

The bull-riding event is about to begin at the Will Rogers Championship Rodeo. Wade waits anxiously at the rail, watching the other riders ready themselves for their rides.

The announcer calls the name of the first cowboy in the event. The gate swings wide and the cowboy is flung from his bull in seconds.

Rodeo expert Will Cook gives Wade a tip: "The bulls like it when you poke your fingers in their ears just like this. . ." SAM JONES

Will Cook, one of the promoters of the rodeo, finds Wade and outfits him with a cowboy hat and spurs. He pulls him behind the pit where the other cowboys are pacing and waiting for their rides.

WILL: Okay, listen, we don't have much time here, so pay attention. When they open that gate, this bull's gonna step to his left. I know him pretty well. When you leave, be stiff. You don't want to be relaxed or he's gonna launch you into tomorrow. You keep your right arm tight against your side and pull hard on the rope. Keep your other arm here in the air and let that sort of guide you. He's gonna try to get away from you, so you just dig your heels into his side. Now, when you get off this bull, you'll still be squeezing the hold with your right hand, but when you feel yourself losing him, open that hand and push him away from you. When you land, roll and get out of there. The main fear of doing this is getting underneath him. You don't want him steppin' on you.

WADE: Keep this hand tight?

"Nice bull . . . good bull
. . . whoaaaaah!" SAM JONES

WILL: TIGHT! You're gonna be fine. You're fourth at this point.

Will jumps up to the gate and sends another rider into the ring. Wade watches over a fence as the rider hangs on until the bell sounds and is finally thrown.

The next rider hangs on for several seconds, but as he starts to slip, his hand sticks in the rope and he is thrown face-first into one of the bull's horns. The rodeo clowns rush to his side and run the bull away. The crowd cheers as the bloodied cowboy rises to his feet and is helped out of the ring.

WILL: Let's go, Wade!

Wade climbs the stand and sees his bull.

Another cowboy goes off with a good ride. The crowd cheers. The rodeo announcer calls Wade's name and two cowboys help him ease onto the bull's back. As he sits down, the bull bucks hard and slams Wade's leg against the side of the pen. Wade looks as if he's going to call it off.

COWBOY: Just settle on down there. You'll be fine.

Wade settles back down and gives the nod. The gate swings wide and the bull, as predicted, steps to his left. Wade holds on for a few bucks, but quickly loses balance and falls. He rolls perfectly, gets to his feet, and scrambles back to the fence. The crowd cheers.

CUT TO:

INTERIOR NEON—NIGHT

The lights of the fair disappearing behind them, the cast rolls back to the motel. Wade talks a mile a minute.

WADE: You should see those guys back there getting ready to ride. Those guys are intense!

BRAD: You gotta be. To ride like they do it, you gotta be intense.

WADE: You should see their faces. You can see in their eyes, like they're in another world. They're just pumping up there. That one guy that got the horn in his face, he was standing there getting pumped . . . he wraps his hand in there and he's rubbing it to get it hot . . .

BRAD: He was putting a suicide grip on there.

WADE: No, he was getting it hot. The stuff on there gets hot and really sticky. And he wrapped it around his wrist. This guy was telling me that if you wrap it around like that and the bull turns into you when you fall, you have a good chance of getting hung. That's when you get hurt. That guy, though, was into it.

BRAD: Those guys ain't scared of shit if they do that there.

WADE: No way. They're scared, they just go through it. You'd be a fool if you weren't scared. That thing'll kill you. Man, what a relief that is.

CHERI: We were totally nervous for you.

WADE: You just can't imagine. I remember

looking up, when I was getting on that thing, and he jumped and slammed my leg. I remember stopping and him saying, "Just ease on down in there." I was just looking out at that crowd and thinking, "No way. This is crazy. What the hell are you doing?" But it was too late. The anticipation of what was going to happen when it came out was just overwhelming. A lot of nerves built up to that.

BRAD: I knew you'd do it.

CHERI: We went on the bumper cars. It was kind of a letdown after the demolition derby.

WADE: I like cowboys, man.

BRAD: Me too. I like that atmosphere.

WADE: They're just a bunch of good ol' boys. It's true.

BRAD: They say what's on their mind. There's no front about it or nothing. They're just honest and clean cut.

WADE: They're real nice people.

FADE OUT.

J.D. mentioned that he heard Brad and Wade had had a wild night. It was something that I would have been better off not knowing. Although I acted like it was no big deal, I felt sick to my stomach.

DAY 13:

TRAVEL: 488 miles/9.2 hours raw drive time

Roll the time back. When you hit New Mexico, you're in Mountain Time.

PLACES OF INTEREST:
- **The Hammond Store,** in Hydro, Oklahoma, has been owned and operated by Lucille Hammond for fifty-odd years.
- **Enterprise Square** at 2501 East Memorial Road in Oklahoma City is a tribute to the free enterprise system. A surreal audio/visual presentation of giant consumer goods and cold, hard cash.
- **The Stockyard** of Oklahoma City is the place to see the beef industry at its most raw. Scrawny animals are driven in and out of their tiny pens and sold at auction—factory meat. From 8 A.M. Monday–Thursday, in the southwest section of the city, at the corner of Agnew Avenue and Exchange Street. (405)235-9301.
- **The Domino Saloon,** in Shamrock, Texas, is a gathering place for locals who sit around and play dominoes all day.
- **Cadillac Ranch,** in Amarillo. Is it art or is it refuse? Ten Cadillacs are buried facedown in the middle of a field. Feel free to stop by and engrave your name into one of the cars for posterity's sake. Just off I-40 east of Amarillo.

PLACES TO EAT:
- The **Big Texan Steak House** in Amarillo has the all-you-can-eat ultimatum—if you can finish one of their 72-ounce steaks, a baked potato, shrimp cocktail, and a roll, it's on the house. On I-40 in Amarillo. (806) 372-7000.

ACCOMMODATIONS:
- **Motel 6,** 1600 Cedar Street, Raton, New Mexico. (505) 445-2777.

FADE IN:
INTERIOR NEON—MORNING

Deciding to make time on a long drive, the gang sets out early for Colorado Springs with Cheri behind the wheel.

CHERI: What's the most embarrassing thing you've ever done?

No one answers.

CHERI: Okay. I'll give you an embarrassing one . . .

WADE: I peed in my pants.

CHERI: You peed your pants?

WADE: I was over at my stepdad's house at Thanksgiving. I was laughing so damn hard . . .

EILEEN: How old were you?

WADE: I think I was a freshman. Someone told a joke and I was laughing so damn hard that I couldn't hold it. I kept trying to stop laughing long enough to get up, but I just couldn't and finally I just lost it. We were sitting at the dinner table, the one where all the kids sit. Only my brother knew about it, so I reached over like I was getting something and knocked my milk into my lap. Everyone thought the milk was what it was.

CHERI: Milk and pee. Nice.

BRAD: I walked right into a column. I was in Atlanta with my boys and we were just walking down the street and I see this girl. So I'm looking at her and I'm drinking this drink and I just went full speed right into that cement column. I mean, my

Up extra early to work out new route with J.D. Bad mood—couldn't get thoughts of Wade and some girl out of my head. Moreover, I felt like a fool, like I meant nothing to him, and that everyone was looking at me like I was so naive to have thought that he really cared. None of this would have been so traumatic, but the Matt scene was keeping my emotions on edge.

drink went all over the place and I just stood there, trying to catch my balance. I was about to fall down. The girl, she was just laughing like crazy.

WADE: Man, look at that spread. It would be cool to work on a ranch, I think. That's what that cowboy last night does.

BRAD: He works on a ranch?

WADE: He owns one. He used to ride on the rodeo circuit. He said you make a lot of money, but you can't do it very long. It's too hard on your body. He quit when he was thirty. Now they have a ranch, him and his family. They run cattle and they run bucking broncs out on the southeastern tip of Oklahoma.

BRAD: I'd like to learn how to ride a horse. I never rode a horse.

WADE: I'd like to learn how to ride one well, like those guys. I just think that would be fun, just be on a horse, working cattle.

BRAD: It would be a free-spirited lifestyle.

WADE: You come down to the corral, some of the dudes are trying to break a horse . . .

BRAD: You ain't got no worries, hardly.

CHERI: You ever see that movie *Children of the Corn?*

WADE: I saw part of it.

CHERI: Kansas reminds me of that. Hey, are we going to get to see the tae kwon do team tomorrow?

BRAD: We're gonna try.

CHERI: What's the difference between karate and Kung Fu?

BRAD: Well, Kung Fu is a lot of movement, like tai chi. Have you ever heard of that?

CHERI: Yeah.

BRAD: It's like that with a lot of grabbing and pulling and things like that. They do kicks all below the waist. What I do is more just fighting. All our kicks are above the waist, like the head and chest.

EILEEN: That's another thing my dad used to make me do, is go see those Kung Fu movies. It was horrible. I would literally turn around in my seat and stare backwards in the theater. I hated it. I was so bored. And usually there would be two of them in a row.

WADE: I loved those. The best one I ever saw was this one called *The Master Killer,* or something. It was awesome. It was about this guy who was a nobody, who wanted to be the best killer. What was cool was that they showed all the things he had to do to make him better. Like, in order to eat, he had to run across this moat that had all these logs floating in it. All the other students were so quick and light-footed they would run across the logs without falling in. Then he comes up, takes his first step, and *bwooosh,* right into the water. And eventually he could do it. Then, to get him stronger, they made him carry buckets of water and they strapped knives around him that were sticking out, so if he lowered his arms he'd stab himself. He'd have to carry buckets of water up this forty-five-degree hill. At first he can barely do it. Then after a while, he's just walking with his hands straight out. He gets so strong that this other guy slips off the pole and he just sticks his leg out and catches him. It was great.

EILEEN: I already feel myself getting sleepy.

Wade opens a copy of *USA Today* to the sports page.

WADE: I can't believe Hardaway is making more than Shaquille O'Neal. That won't last long.

BRAD: Hardaway ain't no franchise. He's good, but he ain't no Shaq.

WADE: He signed for thirteen years for sixty-eight million.

BRAD: Are you sure he's making more than Shaq? That's thirteen years, now.

WADE: It says right here, "Anfernee Hardaway Thursday made Shaquille O'Neal the second highest paid Orlando Magic."

BRAD: Anfernee Hardaway's a punk.

WADE: Wait, listen to this one, "Hardaway's contract is second in the league to Larry Johnson's eighty-four-million dollar deal. Jesus. That's just getting out of hand. Eighty-four million for playing a sport. There's got to be a cap on it sometime. Can you believe that?

BRAD: I didn't know Larry Johnson was making that much.

WADE: Sixty-eight million is amazing in itself, but eighty-four? How do you justify that? How do you afford that?

BRAD: Well, look at ticket sales and look at how many people are watching them play. Think about how much they're making off of

> Wade asked me what was wrong and I told him in brief. He assured me that I didn't have to worry. Although he laughed and gave me a hug, I knew it had ended things between us. He could no longer deal with such neuroticism. I just had to say how I felt and I knew that this was a situation which I could no longer deal with.

Larry Johnson being there. The owner's got to be making three-hundred million off him being there.

WADE: Hey, in Arizona, they're having the top rodeo riders compete in the Coors Series Showdown. That looks fun as hell. I'm ready to go and be a cowboy. I want to do it again. That's the only way to do it, right away, right after you've done it, when you still have that adrenaline.

CHERI: That's how skydiving is, too. You get all nervous.

WADE: Oh my God. Do you know how many years Johnson's contract is? It's only eight years. That means he's making over eight million a year. They're trying to say here that Derrick Coleman's attorney is trying to negotiate one that's more than Larry Johnson's.

BRAD: No way Coleman's as good as Larry Johnson. Michael Jordan was definitely the best player . . . I mean head and shoulders the best player . . . and he was nowhere near the highest paid player.

WADE: But he made so much on endorsements.

BRAD: They said he made like, thirty-eight-million dollars a year on endorsements alone.

WADE: He could have asked for a hundred million and they would have given it to him. He could have been the biggest thing ever.

BRAD: I guess that's good, though. With him not asking for all that money, they could afford to have other players like Scottie Pippen around. See, Orlando shouldn't be able to get too many more players. They got Hardaway and Shaq; they can't afford anyone else who's decent.

Cheri opens a section of the newspaper in front of her as she drives.

CHERI: Is that all you've got, the sports section? Can I have the front page?

WADE: You're not reading the paper while you're driving. No way!

BRAD: She's trying to read the paper while she's driving?

EILEEN: No way!

CHERI: I can read while I drive.

WADE: Not in this car, you can't. Not while I'm in it.

BRAD: You're trying to kill us.

CHERI: All you do is glance down and up.

BRAD: All you do is glance to the hospital. Glance to the funeral home.

CHERI: I used to study on the way to school all the time.

BRAD: That's when you were by yourself. You better not kill me, boy. I know a lot of women in Georgia that'll come after you.

WADE: My mother'll come after you.

> CUT TO:

INTERIOR NEON—AFTERNOON

After a quick lunch stop, the Neon returns to the windy Kansas highway and moves on toward Colorado.

CHERI: *(to Eileen)* Maybe next time we stop you can braid my hair. I can't believe

Stopped at a roadside restaurant in Kansas, Cheri tries the old "pull my finger" gag on the Happy Chef while Eileen awaits the results. SAM JONES

that's coming back in. It's so ugly. I just hope feathering doesn't come back in.

EILEEN: Oh, god. Farrah Fawcett.

CHERI: Did you ever wear your hair like that?

EILEEN: For a little while I did.

CHERI: Man, freshman year of high school. I had all my hair just whooshing back. And then you get it to go together in the back.

EILEEN: And they had those feathers on, like strips of leather that you hung from your hair.

CHERI: Very tacky. It used to take me an hour to do my hair every day, to get all the feathers to go back just right. In eighth grade I went to get a body wave and it came out *so* curly. I just cried. I was so upset. Hey! What are you guys doing, putting cotton in your ears?

BRAD: We don't want to hear this.

CHERI: We had to listen to you talk about basketball! *(to Eileen)* Man, I do *not* want to go back to St. Louis.

EILEEN: Why not?

CHERI: I'm in total denial at this point. I don't want to think about getting a job. I have to figure out what I'm doing and fill out school applications. The bad thing about it is I'll have to explain what I've been doing since I graduated.

EILEEN: How many years since you graduated?

CHERI: Right at three.

EILEEN: I have to work when I get back. I'm having fun, but I feel guilty. And then when I get home all my friends are just going to want to go out.

CHERI: I'm hungry already.

WADE: Me too.

CHERI: Potbelly's restaurant. Maybe we should eat there.

EILEEN: That sounds great. That's the way to get people into your restaurant. It's like Pudgy's Chicken; would you eat it?

CHERI: There's a place in California called Fat Burger.

EILEEN: There's another place in California, a restaurant, that sells bugs.

CHERI: Bugs?

EILEEN: Bugs. And not just chocolate-covered ants. They have crickets and . . .

WADE: The best things are those earthworms. Those things are so good.

CHERI: Oh, gross!

WADE: No, you can dip them in Cajun sauce or barbecue sauce. They dry them out and stretch them out so they're crispy.

CHERI: I would not eat an earthworm.

BRAD: Get your protein, though.

CHERI: I'll get my protein elsewhere, thank you.

WADE: Slugs aren't bad. Pour a little salt on them and watch them dissolve right there in your mouth. Listen to them sizzle. Did you ever do that to a slug?

CHERI: Or take a magnifying glass and burn them up on the sidewalk. Fun in the sun.

WADE: I used to take a mirror and blind

Taking a break on an empty Kansas highway for a seventh-inning stretch. SAM JONES

people when they drove by my house. Just sit out on the porch and catch them right in the eye.

EILEEN: Didn't someone do that on "The Twilight Zone"?

WADE: Yeah.

EILEEN: I love that show. Every year on New Year's day they have a marathon. That's the only time I get to see it anymore.

WADE: I like the old "Star Trek" episodes, too.

BRAD: Oh, man, "Star Trek" is the best.

WADE: Spock is bad, man. Kirk's pretty cool, too, but when it comes right down to it, Spock can kick some ass.

BRAD: Kirk's the man, though. He can kiss anything. He'll be kissing green women, purple women, good god, he gets it all the time. I used to watch "Dallas."

WADE: I never watched any nighttime soaps.

BRAD: I used to love J.R. He couldn't be beat. He'd tear your life apart and laugh about it.

WADE: I remember when he got shot. It was the biggest thing I had ever seen.

BRAD: Yeah, who shot J.R.? They had T-shirts, bumper stickers, all that. I loved him. He would just ruin folks. He was bad. Same thing with Jake on "Days of Our Lives."

CHERI: Jake wasn't on "Days of Our Lives."

BRAD: Oh, yeah, he was on "Another World." He'd be tearin' people up, too.

EILEEN: You sound like a couch potato.

BRAD: In college, when I wasn't working, we used to schedule our classes around "Days of Our Lives" and "Another World."

EILEEN: You guys are so weird.

BRAD: Those two shows came on at one o'clock and two o'clock and nobody would be in class during those hours. That, of course, led right to "Scooby Doo."

WADE: That show was the coolest.

BRAD: Scoobie snacks. They'd always make those sandwiches that were like four feet high and steal them from each other. And Daphne was a babe, man.

WADE: She was, man.

CHERI: I can't believe you talk like that about a cartoon character. Doesn't it ever stop?

BRAD: I wonder whatever happened to that girl who played Blair on "The Facts of Life."

WADE: She got fat as hell.

CHERI: She's big?

WADE: Hell, yeah. All of them swelled up after that show.

BRAD: *(singing)* I think it goes something like "You take the good, you take the bad, you take them both and there you have the facts of life, the facts of life . . ." Then it goes like "There's a time you got to grow and show you're getting older, now you know the facts of life, the facts of life . . ."

EILEEN: Brad, it is so scary that you know the words to that song.

BRAD: *(singing)* "The facts of life are all about youuuuu . . ."

> Sad but relieved.
> Drove all day. Stopped for dinner at an all-you-can-eat country buffet in Kansas—flat, brown, nothing to see, except high winds that made driving very slow. Did a dirt-road drive-by at top speed with Eileen driving—good thing we were buckled in. Almost ran out of gas before we got to Colorado Springs. Arrived at 1:30 A.M. Hellish day. Good night.

WADE: You should have done something with your childhood.

BRAD: *(singing)* "It takes different strokes to move the world, yes it does, it takes different strokes to move the world." . . . Did y'all ever watch that? "Different Strokes?"

EILEEN AND WADE: Yeah.

BRAD: You ever watch "Saved by the Bell"?

CHERI: That's the stupidest show on television.

BRAD: Zack's cool. Zack's cool as the back side of my pillow.

EILEEN: No way.

BRAD: You don't think Zack looks good?

EILEEN: It's Ricky Schroeder syndrome. He looked good when he was younger, but he's just blown up.

CHERI: Did you hear those people say they thought we were on "90210"?

EILEEN: I never liked that show and I never got into "Class of '96."

BRAD: Now that was the best and probably the most realistic show on TV. All that other stuff was silly, but "Class of '96" was more realistic. It was just about people in their freshman year of college and it dealt with girls losing their virginity and guys having to deal with getting dates with girls and having to deal with financial aid and getting part-time jobs. It trips me out how shows that are realistic never make it and shows that are all fantasy make it every damn time. It's like "90210" is so successful and is so full of shit . . .

EILEEN: People have realistic problems in their everyday life. They don't want to see real life on television.

FADE OUT.

DAY 14:

TRAVEL: 285 miles/5.5 hours raw drive time

PLACES OF INTEREST:
- **Taos Pueblo,** Taos, New Mexico. Indian pueblos abound in New Mexico. This one is one of the most pristine. It's two miles north of Taos Plaza, half a mile off Highway 68.
- GUNS, GUNS, GUNS. The largest firing range in America is the **Whittington Center,** which you will pass on your way across New Mexico. Learn how to operate a firearm in Raton, New Mexico. (505) 445-3615.
- **The world's largest Hercules beetle** advertises an exotic insect museum next to U.S. 115, south of Colorado Springs.
- If you're a fan of capital punishment, you may want to visit New Mexico's first electric chair at the **Santa Fe Trail Museum** in Springer, New Mexico.
- Located in Colorado Springs, **The World Rodeo Museum** holds a lot of history of the Old West. 101 Pro Rodeo Drive. (719) 593-8840.
- **Garden of the Gods,** on the west edge of Colorado Springs, off U.S. 24 west at the Ridge Road exit, has an array of spectacular rock formations sculpted by eons of natural erosion. (719) 635-2569.
- **Boulder,** Colorado, is a great college town, full of bookstores, coffeehouses, clubs, and crunchy-granola-type inhabitants.
- For a scenic route, take U.S. 68 north from Taos. Stop at the **Big Pile of Bones and Other Stuff** on the way and pick up a real cigar-store Indian. Continue north to U.S. 522, which turns into U.S. 159 at the Colorado border. Turn east on U.S. 160 and follow it to I-25 North into Colorado Springs.

PLACES TO EAT:
- Try the Rocky Mountain Oysters (bull testicles)
at the **Buckhorn Exchange,** Denver's oldest restaurant, where heads of game cover the walls. 1000
Osage Avenue, Denver. (303) 534-9505.
- **The Fort,** in Morrison, Colorado, still accepts
payment in beaver pelts. They serve up steaks with
an Old West flavor. 19192 Highway 8. (303) 697-4771.
- Even though it's in a shopping center, **Casa Bonita**
isn't just another Mexican restaurant, it's a bona
fide tourist trap. It seats two-thousand and if you
ask for a cliffside table, you'll have a perfect
view of cliff divers jumping from their twenty-
five-foot waterfall. 6715 West Colfax, Denver.
(303) 232-5115.

NIGHTLIFE:
- **The Fox Theater,** on the hill at U.C. Boulder, is a
happening spot. Saturday nights it turns into a
disco inferno. 1135 13th Street. (303) 447-9883.

ACCOMMODATIONS:
- **Estes Park** has several riverside resorts on the
edge of the Rocky Mountain National Park. Try the
National Park Resort. (303) 586-4563.
- **Best Western Movie Manor** in Monte Vista, Colorado
(near Great Sand Dunes), allows you to watch the
next-door drive-in movie from your bed, complete
with a speaker in your room. (719) 852-5921.
- **The Boulderado Hotel** in Boulder is an old-time
Western hotel rumored to be haunted, maybe by the
ghost of Teddy Roosevelt, who once slept here. 2115
13th Street. (303) 442-4344.

FADE IN:
INTERIOR NEON—DAY

Our travelers drive in the morning to the
Olympic Training Center, where they are
taught the arts of shooting and tae kwon do
by the Olympic athletes who are preparing
for the 1996 games.

After lunch at a local Chinese restaurant,
they set out for Estes Park, where they

Brad shows off his form at the Olympic Tae
Kwon Do Center in Colorado Springs. SAM
JONES

will spend the night in a cabin on the edge of the Rocky Mountains.

BRAD: Man, it's nice up here. It'd be nice to have a cabin up here in the woods, lake in the back, chocolate Lab running around . . .

WADE: Why a chocolate Lab, why not a white one?

BRAD: I could have said black Lab. I like chocolate ones. They look better. Or one of those womeraners . . .

WADE: What?

BRAD: You know, it's a dog, a womeraner?

CHERI: A weimaraner. It's a big gray dog.

WADE: Weimaraner? What's that?

BRAD: They use them as hunting dogs.

CHERI: I can't wait to do some rock climbing. That's gonna be cool.

WADE: That's on the schedule in Vegas.

CHERI: I imagine the weather's gonna be pretty nice there, huh?

WADE: It should be nice everywhere once we get further west. I can't wait to get up to the cabin.

CHERI: There might be a hot spring up there that we can get into.

BRAD: I ain't getting into no hot spring. You can get into a hot spring if you want to. Get in there with one of those dinosaurs that didn't die, hiding up there under those hot springs.

Eileen reaches through the seat and kicks Cheri in the shoulder. Cheri looks in the rearview mirror at Brad.

Champion running target shooter Lonn Saunders gives Cheri a few pointers in the 10-meter event. SAM JONES

We shot pistols and then .22 caliber rifles. I did really good with both of them, especially the pistol. I could tell that this really bothered Brad. He hates it when a girl does better than he does.

EILEEN: Cheri looks at Brad right away. I just wanted to see if you were awake. Then I tried to make it look like Brad did it.

BRAD: I'm keeping my hands to myself.

EILEEN: But you look suspicious.

BRAD: I've always been suspicious looking. In school when someone did something, the teacher always looked right at me. Every time something happened—Brad. Something goes wrong at the school, they call me to the office. They wouldn't have a clue who did it. They'd just assume I did it.

CHERI: Have you ever seen such a bunch of losers as high school teachers? Maybe you get lucky and have one or two really good ones, but for the most part . . .

WADE: Yeah, you look back now and it seems that way. Back then, though, they seemed like God.

CHERI: We had this one teacher who was so bad. He would come back from lunch and have food in his mustache and have his pants unzipped. He was just totally out of touch. One day we put someone in the locker. We had twins in our class and one day one of them hid in a locker. So during class he starts pounding and Mr. Neidermier is like, "What's that?" The guy was just clueless. High school was weird.

BRAD: Yeah, all the way up through high school. I'm really surprised that I never got my ass kicked in high school. I used to mess with everybody's girlfriend and talk so much shit and didn't weigh but 132 pounds.

CHERI: Well, Brad, you said that you were going to get more in touch with your sensitive side. What kind of stuff does that include?

Eileen spoke to our waitress in Chinese and it was impressive. We had a tae kwon do demonstration next and they actually had us take our shoes off and participate. We had to yell (grunt) when we performed the moves they showed us and I felt so clumsy. I am sure I didn't look much better.

EILEEN: How are you going to advance toward your goal?

BRAD: I think I made a big step by saying I wanted to change.

CHERI: Yeah, I was really surprised when you said that.

EILEEN: Okay, first step: admission of the problem. Step two?

BRAD: I don't know. I'll just have to tackle things as they arise. I mean, as far as the whole fear thing goes, I can't just say, "Okay, I'm scared now."

EILEEN: Why?

BRAD: It's just not how I was raised.

CHERI: I can understand that, just seeing the way your dad is. His personality really comes through in you.

BRAD: Yeah. I was raised not to be afraid of anything.

CHERI: But everyone is afraid of something. Even those bull riders.

BRAD: I see my dad, as he's getting older, he's getting softer. When I was young, like in grade school, my dad was the toughest guy everybody knew. He wasn't mean, but very strict.

CHERI: Were you scared of him?

BRAD: Yes. Most definitely.

CHERI: So, if you broke something you were scared you would get a whipping?

BRAD: Scared to death. Most of the times I did. If I broke something, my dad would make sure it would never happen again. My grandfather keeps telling me how me and my dad are so much alike, when he was my age.

He tells me that when my dad was my age, he used to think he could stick his finger in the ground and turn the Earth. And my dad doesn't even go hunting anymore.

CHERI: Does that change the way you look at things?

BRAD: Kind of, but it's hard, considering that he raised me for twenty-one years to be the other way. But, I'm just trying not to be so hard on other people.

Wade stares pensively out the window while Cheri drives.

CHERI: What's been bumming you out today?

WADE: It's just one of those days I want to be quiet.

CHERI: I know a guy with a place in Aspen.

WADE: It must be great to live up there.

CHERI: That's where everyone was boy-cotting because of the homosexual issue.

WADE: Boycotting what?

CHERI: Aspen. Everything. A lot of the stars go to Aspen. I don't know if it was just in that county or what, but they wanted to make a law saying that there was to be no special laws for homosexuals, that it was unconstitutional. So a lot of the stars were boycotting in Aspen. That was last year.

Cheri takes the wheel after a pit-stop during the drive to Estes Park. SAM JONES

WADE: It's so gloomy here. Everywhere we've gone in the last two days has been so gloomy. It's like we're in this dome of gloom.

CHERI: Here they get sunshine three hun-dred days a year, so we have pretty bad tim-ing. This is just like, blah.

Our cabin is amazing. We have everything we need—a fireplace, a kitchen—it's split-level and clean.

CUT TO:

EXTERIOR CABIN IN ESTES PARK—EVENING

They arrive at the cabin and Brad opens the door. He hesitates at the doorway.

WADE: Get in there. What are you, chicken?

BRAD: I ain't no chicken, but I ain't gonna walk right into no dark room, either.

EILEEN: Wow, this is huge.

CHERI: Indoor plumbing.

BRAD: All right women, y'all get into the kitchen and fix me up something to eat.

CHERI: Shut up.

EILEEN: Oh, Brad, give it a rest.

BRAD: There's only two places for y'all. Y'all are in the bedroom, get on into the kitchen.

EILEEN: Are you watching television?

BRAD: "Cagney and Lacey."

CHERI: I'm sure we came all the way up here to watch TV. Turn it off.

CUT TO:

INTERIOR CABIN—NIGHT

After dinner, the cast settles in front of the fire while Wade makes Jiffy Pop popcorn on the stove.

WADE: When I was a kid, I used to think this stuff was so cool. I guess I still do.

EILEEN: I remember seeing those commercials on television, when the whole family is cooking their Jiffy Pop.

CHERI: Then microwave popcorn came along and blew it away.

EILEEN: Anyone know any stories? I love scary stories.

CHERI: It's best when you're around a campfire and it's dark and you've got total darkness behind you.

WADE: My mother used to tell us a story about a bear that lived up on the hill right by our house.

BRAD: My grandma used to tell us a story like that.

CHERI: Wait, what happened with the bear?

WADE: All these men would come walking through the woods one by one and this bear would get them all until it was me, my mom, my brother, and our dog, Stubby, which was the dog we had forever.

BRAD: Same story! Same damn story my grandma used to tell us.

WADE: Then my grandpa would come riding up on this horse and get the bear, just before he got us.

BRAD: That story, I can promise you my grandma told us the same exact story when I was little. But she used to make her voice real deep and she would talk like the grizzly bear and all. Me and my cousin used to sit on the porch listening to her and she used to scare us to death!

CHERI: My grandma used to tell us stories like that, but we'd be running away and one of us would lose our shoe and we'd all panic.

BRAD: See, we would always get it. The bear would always get one of us in the end.

Huge snowflakes fell from the sky so we ran around catching them in our mouths. After dinner we made S'mores and popcorn—hung out by the fire, wrote postcards, told slumber party stories, and had a big pillow fight. Today was a blast.

One of the kids. She'd be the bear and grab us and scare us. Used to make my dad mad because he didn't want us to be scared of anything, so she used to do it just to get his goat. You could see it, though, when he would come and get us, that he was mad. She would do that all the time.

WADE: Sometimes the bear would get Stubby, and that's when I would get upset. I used to love to have that scared feeling. When I was a kid I used to go over to my friend's house when his parents went out for the night. He would have a baby-sitter. This one guy . . . we used to turn off all the lights in the whole house and he would come after us. You'd be hiding and he'd be walking through the house looking for you. Man, you could feel your heart beating right through your chest.

BRAD: My dad used to do something to me when I was little that used to scare me. He used to put his whole hand over my face and I couldn't breathe. And he would do it at like two o'clock in the morning. I would be in my bed, asleep.

WADE: WHAT!?

BRAD: He would sneak out of his bed . . .

EILEEN: Why would he do that?

BRAD: He thought it was funny.

CHERI: No wonder you turned out like this.

BRAD: Serious. He would sneak out of bed and crawl into my room and hide under the bed. He would reach his arm out and . . . Bam! Grab me. I would wake up and not be able to breathe. I would be bawling. And my mom would come in and let him have it. He just thought it was funny. He did that until I was big enough to hear him coming.

WADE: That's when you wait for him with a bat. He should be beat for that.

EILEEN: That's nuts.

BRAD: That's why I didn't come in here when it was dark. I always stop first and look.

WADE: I would be scarred for life. The fear of the man from under the bed. Before this trip's over I'll have to sneak over to your side of the room and get him.

BRAD: He used to do stuff like that to me all the time, to test to see if I was scared of anything.

WADE: My uncle would torment me. He would take my grandmother's nylons and pull them over his face and get me in the bedroom and shut the door. He would walk around with his arms out like a zombie and just follow me really slow. I would run out of the room and he would just follow me, real slow. He wouldn't even run, making that noise . . . "Uhhhhhnnnnnn."

BRAD: I try to scare my little cousins sometimes, but you just can't scare them anymore.

FADE OUT.

DAY 15:

Sunday, October 10:

Estes Park, CO, to Moab, UT

Travel: 378 miles/ 7.7 hours raw drive time

PLACES OF INTEREST:
- For a taste of the truly bizarre, check out the **Baldpate Inn** before you leave Estes Park. It's home to the key to Hitler's Berchtesgaden bomb shelter. 4900 Highway 7. (303) 586-6151.
- **Bull Whacker** casino in Blackhawk, Colorado. In the Old West, ranch hands and cowboys had nowhere to spend their wages, so they would take their earnings into town and blow it all in a wild weekend. Today, the scene is much the same in the low-stakes gambling halls of this small town, except that you can expect to see a lot more polyester.
- **The Buffalo Bill Museum** on Lookout Mountain just outside Golden, Colorado, exhibits artifacts from Bill Cody's careers as an Indian scout, buffalo hunter, and Wild West Show proprietor. Three miles south of I-40 off Lookout Mountain Road. (303) 526-0747.

ACCOMMODATIONS:
- **Arches National Park**, near Moab, has some of the most scenic camping in the country. Natural red and yellow sandstone arches and spires rise from the desert floor. Camp out.
- **Super 8 Motel,** 889 North Main Street, Moab. (801) 259-8868.

FADE IN:
INTERIOR NEON—MORNING

After a pancake breakfast and a quick shopping tour of Estes Park, the cast once
again loads up and starts for Moab, Utah.

As they pull out, the four sit in agitated
silence.

WADE: (*to Eileen*) I don't understand why
it's such a big deal for you to sit behind
me when you know his legs are so long
they're not going to fit.

EILEEN: Well, I know his legs are longer,
but it's not like I'm comfortable, either.

WADE: So a person whose legs are like a
foot longer ... who's going to be more comfortable?

EILEEN: Couldn't we take turns, though?

WADE: Why should he sit behind me or me sit
behind him and have our legs pushed into
our chest?

BRAD: Cheri never questions it.

CHERI: I sat behind Wade a million times.
You're being ridiculous.

WADE: (*to Cheri*) When's the last time you
talked to your mom?

CHERI: I talked to her yesterday morning
for the first time since we left, so I talked
to her for forty-five minutes.

WADE: You called her from the hotel?

CHERI: Yeah. I called her collect and had
her call me back. I gave her all the scoops.
I always ask her advice when I'm stuck on
something. My mom's into reading self-help

> Cameras woke us up—thinking that
> they would catch us in a
> compromising position, but the
> guys were in one bed and we
> (Eileen and I) were in the other.

books and getting to know yourself and all that. She's in tune with things like that.

WADE: Wow. You didn't talk to her since Boston?

CHERI: Well, I talked to my dad the other day for just five minutes. I didn't want to say much because usually they'll both get on at the same time so I can talk to both of them. If I call in the middle of the night, my mom's the type who won't remember the conversation. And my dad's in Biloxi right now.

WADE: Doing what?

CHERI: Fishing. He goes fishing a lot. Him and a bunch of guys go every year for a week.

WADE: What does he do?

CHERI: He works for the Defensive Mapping Agency Aerospace Center. They make maps and plot geographical points for guided missiles and stuff like that.

WADE: What's his position?

CHERI: He does different things, but it all has to do with these maps. I've only been to his work once. They had an open house. It was the only time I was ever there, because it's all top secret.

Cheri picks up a marketing textbook that Eileen has brought with her.

CHERI: Did you get any studying done?

EILEEN: Not much.

CHERI: When I was in school I took some cool classes. Like when I took History of South Africa, it was so funny. None of us knew anything about it and I think a lot of

I have a feeling Wade doesn't think that Matt and me are going to break up when I get home, but that's only because he doesn't know me that well.

people took it because they thought it would be a blow-off class. The teacher would be like, "The Zulus and the Xhosa . . . say it with me." No one could pronounce it. It was really cool learning about it because I had no idea why the whites ran it and why there was all that factional fighting. I took Twentieth-Century Europe, which was really cool, because I took that back in '87, right when they were about to break out of communism. Gorbachev had just taken power and was talking about the five-year plan to freedom. Everyone thought it was so impossible, and then it happened. Everyone was like, "There's no way they're going to drop communism."

EILEEN: I took Nuclear Power and Nuclear Weapons. It was cool because, like you said, nobody knew what was happening. They had minute-by-minute what was happening at Chernobyl and Three Mile Island.

CHERI: What else did I take? I took a weightlifting class. The guy who taught it was in competition. He was preparing for competition and he said he would teach us nutrition if we wanted to go through it with him. So I did it intensely for two and a half months. I didn't drink, I didn't do anything. I worked out and watched my food. Then when it was over everything was all McDonald's and beer.

EILEEN: I'm just getting ready for the big one. I know senior year is full of résumés and interviews and all that.

CHERI: I know. That sucks so bad.

EILEEN: I'm not going to be into it.

CHERI: You have to go into these places and act all excited. My advice to you is to

The guys kept making fun of Eileen. She almost cried. Later she explained that she was sick of them telling her what to do, so she was protesting. That was the first time that I've seen Eileen mad. I used to think that nothing really bothers her, but I'm beginning to realize that she keeps everything inside.

act extremely excited and act like you really want the job if there's even a remote chance that you want it. I went to a couple where I went in and they described it and I just said, "Thanks, but I don't think it's something that I really want." Then I had a couple of second interviews for things that I really wanted. One of them I didn't get and I was really upset. I asked them why and they said that I lacked interest.

EILEEN: I've heard that they can ask really weird questions. Have you been asked any weird ones?

CHERI: Yeah, it can be strange. I've walked into interviews where they just sit back and say, "So, tell us about yourself." And that's the whole interview. So you have to go through your whole background, your schooling, your interests, and why you're interested in the company, with no guidance at all.

EILEEN: I've heard that they'll do things like have a locked window and ask you to open it. And they'll set it up so you can't open it and watch how you deal with it.

CHERI: They're usually not like that. They don't want to torture you.

EILEEN: People have been asked things like, "If you could be a vegetable, what would you be and why?" or "How many pineapples do you think are consumed in the United States every year?" Just to see how you think.

CHERI: One time I was handed a paper clip and told, "Sell this to me." So I had to go through this thing like, "Well, it's better than staples because you're not putting holes in your papers . . . " I couldn't believe they asked me that. Usually they're not like that, though. A lot of times the hardest question is, "Where do you want to be in five years?"

EILEEN: I've heard that a lot of them ask that.

CHERI: As if you have any idea when you're just graduating. What I do is have an interview packet. I took all the standard questions they ask and wrote down answers, so when I go on an interview, I look over all my answers. Like, one question they always ask is, "What's your greatest weakness?" You always say a weakness and turn it into a positive. For instance, you say, "I don't have any experience, but that means I haven't picked up any bad habits and I pick up on things quickly." Whatever you say, don't say something like, "I procrastinate." They'll crucify you.

EILEEN: I'm so used to school and I know that, *bam,* I'm going to be out there.

CHERI: That's one thing I feel about school, that they did nothing to prepare you for the real world at all.

WADE: If someone asked me, "How many pineapples are sold in a year?" I'd just say, "If that's what you want to know, I'm not right for this job."

BRAD: I applied for the Georgia State Patrol and the Georgia Bureau of Investigations. That's plainclothes, D.A.'s office. I applied for the red-dog squadron. The Atlanta city police has this red-dog squadron and all they do is bust in on crack houses and stuff like that. Those interviews are tough. The first one is okay. They

just ask you about yourself. Then they get
more formal. There's five agents behind a
desk and you're just sitting by yourself.
They put a spotlight on you like you're
being interrogated and they just fire questions at you. Real tough questions. Like,
"You're undercover and you're on your way
to make a bust and you pass by a liquor
store and some guy is robbing the store.
What are you going to do?" Are you going to
interfere with the robbery, or are you
going to act like nothing's wrong? And you
don't know if there's a right or wrong
answer to that. If you say you're not going
to interfere with it and the guy has someone at gunpoint . . . you're a cop and you're
kind of going against your principles. But
if you go after him and you jeopardize
months and months of undercover work,
you're undermining the authority. I said I
would keep going and try to call somebody
to come and take care of the robbery.

WADE: You don't have to get them all
right, do you? I mean, part of it is how you
carry yourself, right?

BRAD: Right. But then they watch you. They
do a background check. They come into your
old high school, your colleges . . .

WADE: I had to have that done. When I was
in the Air Force, I had to get the highest
security clearance for the communications
stuff that I saw. Background, everything. I
had tried marijuana and all this stuff
before that.

BRAD: I put down that I tried it once.

WADE: But if I had said that, I wouldn't
have gotten that position.

BRAD: Yeah. And for me, the process is so

slow. When I get home, I could find out I've been hired by one of them. It's a waiting game. It drives you crazy.

EILEEN: *(to Cheri)* When you took marketing, did you have to make up your own product?

CHERI: No, because I just took a basic marketing class.

EILEEN: In ours, everyone in the class had to come up with their own new product. A lot of people came up with things that were already out there, like toothbrushes with toothpaste already in them, but they already have that. Some were really cool, though. One person came up with a Stair-Master you could do while you were sitting down at your desk. One girl wanted to do advertising on the back of bathroom stalls, so all that time isn't wasted.

CHERI: Do you go out clubbing at school?

EILEEN: Yeah, there are some cool bars and clubs around B.C. There's one street where most of them are. They have alternative clubs and dance clubs and all that.

CHERI: Do you have trouble getting in?

EILEEN: Not usually, because I have my sister's ID. She's twenty-five. I have to get a new one, though. I mean it works perfectly when she's not there, but if we go out together, there's an obvious problem.

CHERI: When I was in school I knew these three girls who all used one girl's sister's ID. And they didn't look anything alike. They would all go in as Cheryl Campbell.

EILEEN: There was one bar we went to a lot and I got to know the manager pretty well, except that he knew me by my sister's name, Patricia, but all my friends would come up to me and be like, "Hey, Eileen." He was confused at first, but I think he caught on. I would be talking to my friends and he would go, "Patricia!" and I wouldn't respond. Then he would come up and tap me and go, "Patty!" And I would be like, "Oh, yeah, hi!"

CHERI: I remember sitting out in the car, trying to memorize the names and dates on fake IDs.

EILEEN: And figuring all the stuff they ask you, like, "What sign are you?"

CHERI: I carded this guy one time and he goes, "I left it out there in the parking lot," which is a far walk. So I go, "Okay, when did you graduate high school?" Because he said he was twenty-three. He goes, "I don't know, I didn't." So I say, "When did you graduate grammar school?" He goes, "1987." And I'm like, "Man, you were in there for fifteen years? Either you're dumb or you're lying."

BRAD: I was with a friend of mine, Tony, in Atlanta one time. He was using our friend Cory's Army ID. We all got in and Tony was right behind me. I mean, the bouncer believed the ID, but he had been in the Army, too. So he was just rappin' with Tony, just talking to him. He goes, "I'm in the reserves. Where are you stationed, man?" I see Tony go, "Um, umm . . ." I just started laughing. Finally he goes, "Virginia." And the bouncer's like, "There ain't no Army base in Virginia. It's a Navy base." I was just crying. And the bouncer kept the ID. Tony was like, "I can't get back on the base without that." The other

Brad found out that two of his friends had been killed in a car wreck. I didn't know what to say to him or how to comfort him. He was mad and started slamming things around. He masks his hurt with anger—always afraid that he won't appear manly.

guy was like, "You don't even know where your base is!" It was hysterical.

WADE: I never went into bars. I never could get in.

BRAD: Bouncers are serious in Atlanta. If you get in a fight in Atlanta, you're going to jail. If you even push . . . if there's a lick thrown . . . the bouncers are going to get you. And then there's usually cops right outside the clubs waiting to take you down. Now in Athens, which is right down the road, it's a college town and they got all kinds of bars there. And there you never go to jail. On any given night, you know there's going to be a brawl and the only thing you gotta worry about is the bouncers. And all they'll do is kick you out.

CHERI: What they started doing in Missouri is keeping your picture on file. You couldn't get away with it there.

BRAD: I could use anything. White bouncers just didn't pay attention. I could use *any-body's* black ID. It could look nothing like me. It could say I was thirty-five. Seriously. They wouldn't even question it whatsoever.

CHERI: There was a bar at my school, it was called Whispers. They sent out this flyer that said, "Come to Whispers. Plenty of hot, horny, drunk women." They got closed down within a week for putting that flyer out. How stupid is that?

WADE: *(laughing)* Jesus! Did you ever go there?

EILEEN: Cheri was one of the hot, horny, drunk women.

CHERI: Hey!

Although we have gotten to know a lot about each other, we each know only part—only what each of us wants to be known about ourselves. It's only the part we project, so sometimes I'm skeptical...

EILEEN: My best friend goes to school at Fordham, in the Bronx. She goes out to these bars where people get stabbed and shot . . . that's crazy. She's totally used to hearing gunshots and stuff. I'll be talking to her on the phone and I'll hear sirens and everything. She's like, "Oh, somebody probably just got shot." I'm like, "You're so relaxed." She's like, "Come visit me." And I'm like, "No, you come visit me."

CHERI: Wade, did you have a baby face?

WADE: Yeah. I just looked really young. When I shave, everybody thinks I'm younger than I am. Everybody guesses at least two years younger than I really am. Plus I could never get a good fake ID. My brother was lucky. He's had my ID since he was eighteen.

                                        CUT TO:

INTERIOR NEON—NIGHT

They stop for dinner and return to the road with Eileen driving and the guys in the back seat, where they quickly fall asleep.

CHERI: *(to Eileen)* I didn't mean to jump in earlier with them yelling at you.

EILEEN: I think it was just . . . you know . . .

CHERI: It's just everything.

EILEEN: Then I just felt like it was one against three.

CHERI: Not very good odds there.

FADE OUT.

DAY 16:

Travel: 350 miles/7 hours raw drive time

PLACES OF INTEREST:
- **Hole in the Rock.** Albert Christensen spent
twelve years digging into the side of a mountain.
The result is a fourteen-room home that has become a
major tourist stop in Moab, Utah. South Highway 191.
(801) 686-2250.
- **Monument Valley,** on the way to Kayenta, takes you
through the most scenic landscapes the country has
to offer.

→ **MOUNTAIN BIKING.** Moab is considered the world
capital of this sport. **Slickrock Trail** is the most
popular half-day route. It's a challenging, ten-
mile loop over tremendous sandstone knobs with
views of the La Sal Mountains and the Colorado
River. Rent a bike at Poison Spider Bike Shop in
Moab. 497 North Main Street. (801) 259-7882.

ACCOMMODATIONS:
- **Greyhills Inn** in Tuba City, Arizona, is a Native
American-run hostel-like stayover. (602) 283-6271.
- **Holiday Inn,** Kayenta, Arizona. (602) 697-3221.

FADE-IN:
INTERIOR NEON—AFTERNOON

After spending the morning mountain biking
on Slickrock Trail in Moab with Chuck
Nichols, proprietor of Poison Spider Bike
Shop, our fatigued travelers stop for lunch
at a cafe in Moab.

The cast met up with Adrian Van Deusen at a lunch stop in Moab. After lunch, Adrian continued his journey by bike from Portland, OR, to Santa Fe, NM. SAM JONES

After eating, they load up and head south toward Arizona and the Navajo Indian Reservation.

WADE: I finally found that book I was telling you about with all the questions.

EILEEN: Is this going to be a morality test?

BRAD: I told y'all before and now we're gonna see that you don't have any morals at all.

WADE: Let me find a good one: If you were to die this evening, with no opportunity to communicate with anyone, what would you most regret not telling someone? Why haven't you told them?

Long pause.

WADE: Nobody?

CHERI: I know what I would do. I would regret not telling my brother how much I admire him and how highly I think of him.

WADE: She's gonna start bawling!

CHERI: I am not!

WADE: I see the tears welling up!

BRAD: What would bother me is . . . I don't want to talk about it or I might start bawling.

CHERI: See? It's not just me.

BRAD: I just can't say it or I'll start bawling up. I'd just like to tell Lauren that I love her. All the time we spent together meant the world to me and I really care for her a lot. She means everything to me. And I feel like if I can't have her, this world won't be worth living in anyway.

EILEEN: I wish I'd fallen in love. I've never been in love.

BRAD: I wish I had the balls to tell her I still love her.

EILEEN: I think mine would be a family thing. With a lot of my friends, like when they're on the phone, every conversation ends with, "I love you." I just don't say it as much like I mean it. I would tell my family that I love them.

WADE: You don't tell your family that you love them?

EILEEN: I do, but not that much. I expect them to know it.

CHERI: I can say it to my mom and dad real easily, but I have trouble telling my brother. Okay, question number two.

WADE: Walking along an empty street, you find a wallet that contains $5,000 and no identification. What do you do? Would it alter your decision if there was ID and a picture of either a wealthy-looking young man or a frail old woman? If I came upon $5,000 cash with no name or nothing, it's mine.

I'm really starting to wonder about Wade's intelligence level. I never purposely try to make him look stupid, he does that on his own.

CHERI: Immediately.

BRAD: No question about that.

CHERI: I'd look around, make sure nobody saw me and bolt.

WADE: Me and my best friend found $2,700 one time. We were juniors in high school. We were at this mall called Lloyd Center.

EILEEN: I've heard of that place. I think I've been there. Is that the one with the skating rink?

WADE: Yeah. There's two of them. It was during Christmas time. We were in this expensive men's store, just looking around. I tried on this leather jacket that was on the rack and my friend goes, "Is there something in that pocket?" So I put my hand in there and there was an envelope. I pulled it out and shoved it in my pants. I didn't even look at it. We looked around a little more, but there was no one around. We were a little scared, because this mall, before they remodeled it, was like, drug town.

CHERI: So someone was making a deal?

WADE: That's what we thought. So we walk out and go in the bathroom and I open the envelope. I'm like, "Frank, there's a bunch of money in here!" So we go out to the car and we're totally paranoid that someone's following us. As soon as we start driving, I whip it out and there's twenty hundred-dollar bills and a bunch of fifties in there. We were just sitting there with it fanned out, looking at it. It was amazing. I went home and told my mom the whole story and she was like, "Wade, you have to keep it for a while to see if someone runs an ad in the paper or something." So I held on to it for about a month and . . . nothing.

CHERI: The tough part is if there's ID, though.

EILEEN: Once you attach it to someone. Then it's really like stealing. You'd have to give it back.

CHERI: And hope they give you a reward.

WADE: Okay, here's a real good one. Listen to this: You and a person you love deeply are placed in separate rooms with a

The living room at Albert Christensen's Hole in the Rock cave dwelling outside Moab. It took twelve years for Albert to dig his home into the side of a mountain, and he only lived there for five years before dying. His wife, Gladys, opened the cafe and gift shop that still service the 40,000 visitors who stop in every year. SAM JONES

button . . . who thinks of these questions? With a button next to each of you. You both know that you will both be killed unless someone pushes one of the buttons within sixty minutes. Furthermore, whoever pushes their button first will save the other one, but will be immediately killed. What would you do?

BRAD: So both of you are going to die, or just one?

EILEEN: Well both of you are going to die if no one pushes it, but only one dies if someone pushes it.

WADE: Whoever pushes it first dies, but the other one lives. And if nobody pushes it, you both die. I'd push it.

EILEEN: What would your life be like if you wimped out? I'd push it.

CHERI: I wouldn't want to live with the guilt. Brad?

BRAD: It would depend on who the person was. If it was my parents or Lauren? Definitely.

WADE: Can you urinate in front of another person?

CHERI: Yeah. I had to for drug testing. They sit and watch you.

BRAD: In athletics you do that all the time.

WADE: Would you accept a lifetime allowance of $50,000 a year, adjusted annually for inflation, if accepting it meant that you could never again earn money from work or investments?

CHERI: Does that mean you get $50,000 and

Hole in the Rock—just outside of Moab. I couldn't believe that someone lived in the side of a rock. A whole house carved into the side of a mountain like a cave. It's now a gift shop/tourist trap, a kind of modern-day stone-age Flintstone situation. Bizarre.

you wouldn't have to work at all? Or is it whatever work you do, you'd get $50,000?

WADE: You just get it. You could do whatever you wanted.

CHERI: So you'd never be rich . . .

EILEEN: But you'd have enough.

CHERI: You'd have enough to do all kinds of things. You could do stuff like this all the time, just travel from city to city.

EILEEN: Yeah, I think I would.

BRAD: I don't think I would.

WADE: You should think about it, man. Police don't make more than that, anyway.

BRAD: I know, but I still wouldn't. I'd rather work.

CHERI: You could do volunteer work.

BRAD: But there's a different motivation to work when you make money.

CHERI: There's motivation behind volunteer work. There's satisfaction.

BRAD: I would rather work. I wouldn't do it. I wouldn't want a handout. I'd want to do it my own damn self.

WADE: So winning the lottery is a handout?

BRAD: I don't play the lottery. I don't believe in it.

CHERI: Let me see the book. Let me find a good one. Okay. You've arranged an evening with a friend, but the evening before your date, something comes up which will be much more exciting. How do you handle it?

WADE: I'd just call them and tell them I had something come up.

The cast absorbs the beauty of Utah on the way to Kayenta, AZ. SAM JONES

Wade and Brad were irate! "We don't get to sleep, they don't care if we get to eat, I'm losing muscle tissue, woe is me..." For two grown boys, they sounded like babies.

CHERI: Okay, let me put a spin on it. Say you're going on a date and you're not really crazy about the person and then someone calls you and tells you that there's a huge party going on and all your friends are going to be there.

WADE: I'd think of an excuse.

BRAD: I'd go on the date. I don't break a date.

EILEEN: Then just bring your date and if he turns out to be a loser, lose him.

CHERI: I think I'd duck out.

BRAD: I'd be on my word. If I said I'd go on a date with someone, I'd go on the date. I don't give a damn whatever came up.

Brad stares into the abyss on Slickrock Trail. SAM JONES

WADE: No way. If there was some big party in Atlanta and you had a date with some girl and you knew Chrissy was going to be there and all that . . .

BRAD: I wouldn't go.

WADE: Bullshit! Look at you.

BRAD: That's something about me. If I say I'm gonna do something and I give my word, I'm gonna do it. I mean, you saw in Atlanta, when I said I was going to meet my friends . . . they waited for me in the cold for almost an hour. Someone who was there said, "Let's go, he's probably with that girl. He's not going to show." And my friends said, "No, we're gonna wait. He said he was coming and unless something happened, he's coming." They know that when I give my word, I keep it. End of discussion. Next question.

While the others went biking, Eileen took a photographic look at nearby Arches National Park. EILEEN CHUNG

WADE: Okay, my turn. You are given the power to kill people simply by thinking of their death and twice repeating the word "good-bye." They would die natural deaths and nobody would suspect you. Are there any situations in which you would use this power?

CHERI: Yeah. Mercy killings. If I knew someone really wanted to die and was in misery, I'd do it.

WADE: I'd do it. I'd have done it with Saddam Hussein when the war started.

BRAD: That's one thing I wouldn't have done. I think no man has the right to play God.

WADE: We lost too many lives because of that bastard.

BRAD: Nobody twisted Bush's arm to send our men over there. So why kill Saddam?

WADE: Why? Because he's a terrorist.

BRAD: What gives you the right to kill him, though?

CHERI: He's psycho.

WADE: If I was over there with a gun and was fighting for this country, I would kill him. We tried to kill him.

BRAD: That doesn't mean it's right.

WADE: That means you don't believe in us going to war about anything.

BRAD: I wouldn't.

WADE: You would never go and get involved in anything?

BRAD: Not in a war.

EILEEN: What if we were going to be taken over by another country?

BRAD: Unless it immediately affected my family or my friends, I would not kill

someone. I don't believe in taking anybody's life because some man sitting in the
White House tells me to kill him, because
he tells me he's my enemy.

WADE: If our country didn't get involved
in the wars that they did, you wouldn't
even be sitting here right now.

BRAD: I would not take another man's life
just because the president told me to take
his life. I'm too strong in my religious
convictions to do that. The only way I
would take another man's life is if it
immediately threatened my life or the life
of someone close to me.

CHERI: Isn't that selfish?

BRAD: That is not selfish. I'd kill somebody if they had a gun and they were threatening someone right in front of me and
there was no other way out of it. Other than
that, I wouldn't do it.

WADE: We would not have our freedom if we
had not killed. We would not be a free country. World War I, World War II . . .

BRAD: . . . Vietnam, Korea . . .

CHERI: What about the Civil War?

BRAD: What about it?

CHERI: They had to pick up guns to get the
freedom for the blacks, the North did.

BRAD: That's not what the war was about.
It had something to do with it, but a small
part. It was a small part of Lincoln's
plan.

WADE: It surprises me that someone who
stands for justice and wants to uphold
peace . . .

BRAD: And I do. I'm going to be a cop, but
I'm not going to kill someone just because

someone tells me to. I don't see how you can be so quick to take somebody's life and play God, either.

WADE: You're not seeing the big picture. We wouldn't be sitting in this car right now if we didn't kill people.

BRAD: You mean to tell me that you'd kill somebody over this car? I put a greater value on life, regardless of communist or whoever.

EILEEN: But then you'd have to listen to the communists tell you what to do.

BRAD: I still wouldn't take somebody's life.

CHERI: You still have to consider the quality of life.

BRAD: Y'all don't realize how precious life is. I would not take anybody's life. I would be enslaved before I took somebody's life. If you believe in the Bible and Jesus Christ, it'll tell you that whatever is done to you will be returned to him. You let God take care of it.

WADE: It doesn't work like that.

BRAD: Maybe not in this life, but he'll get it somewhere down the road.

WADE: This is what bothers me about that. You choose to live in this country and par-take in its freedom and everything else but you will not fight for it. You'll let every-one else go and fight for it.

BRAD: That's what this country is all about. It gives me that choice and I choose not to do it. Besides, if you want to look at that, my ancestors built half this damn country, so I shouldn't have to fight for shit!

EILEEN: I don't like that, like we owe you something.

BRAD: You don't worry about that. You don't have to figure you owe me nothing. I'll take what's mine. I don't owe this country anything. I'd say we're even.

CHERI: How do you figure your ancestors relate that to you?

BRAD: They're my people!

CHERI: That's the attitude I don't like that a lot of blacks have.

BRAD: That's the attitude they're supposed to have. I should have been a prince back in Africa, sitting up there running things.

EILEEN: Let's say Saddam bombed the United States. That includes your family, your friends, and you.

BRAD: If he would have, we would have crossed that bridge when we came to it.

WADE: So wait for it?

BRAD: You don't know what's going to happen. You can't read that man's mind. You believe what Bush told you. You believe the propaganda.

WADE: I spent too much time in the military.

BRAD: There were blacks over there dying and it's just modern-day slavery, like Chuck D. said, "They're just modern-day slaves, fighting for the white man."

WADE: That's about the most racist attitude I've ever heard.

BRAD: That's not racist. Because I don't want to go down for Bush?

EILEEN: That's not Bush, it's the whole country.

WADE: I have no doubt that wars mean money. I have no doubt that that was part of the reason we got into the whole thing. But at the same time, you're talking about someone whose goal is to take over the world.

BRAD: There you go, believing propaganda. That's what Bush tells you. He wasn't even thinking about America. Bush jumped into that for money and oil and he knew he'd get everybody riled up by using propaganda and saying, "He's another Hitler. He's gonna try to take over the world." And everybody here's like, "Oh, yeah, let's get him. All the rag-heads, let's kill 'em." All these weak-minded people. Kill for it.

CHERI: Okay, let's say there's a serial killer and you're a cop and you find him. He doesn't have a weapon, so he's not immediately threatening your life, but he's getting away and the only way you can stop him is to kill him. Would you?

BRAD: No. If he didn't have a weapon, I wouldn't kill him.

CHERI: He's going to go off and kill someone right away.

BRAD: I wouldn't kill him. I can't. I'd shoot him in the leg.

WADE: I'd blow him away.

BRAD: That's the way you feel about human life.

WADE: He's taken twenty lives.

BRAD: But two wrongs don't make a right. An eye for an eye just leaves everybody blind.

FADE OUT.

This "showbiz" stuff was not normal to us. No one had warned us about any of the production side of this trip.

DAY 17:

Travel: 70 miles/ 1.2 hours raw drive time

PLACES OF INTEREST:
- **The Navajo Nation** is the largest Indian reservation in the United States, covering 17.5 million acres. In fact, you're soaking in it.
- You'll drive through **The Painted Desert,** one of the Southwest's most beautiful landmarks, on the way to the Grand Canyon.
- **Dinosaur Tracks** were left when the beasts trod this once-tropical area some 200 million years ago. On U.S. 89 the tracks come within a hundred feet of the road.

→ **MORE CAMPING!** Roll out those sleeping bags. You can stay at the **Mather Campground** on the South Rim of the Grand Canyon. It's located just a mile west of Yavapai Lodge. Please don't feed the animals.

PLACES TO EAT:
- Stock up at the Yavapai general store and have yourselves a barbecue at the campground.
- **The Best Western Inn** has an inexpensive, all-you-can-eat dinner. It's outside the Park in the village of Tusayan. (602) 638-2681.
- **Yavapai Lodge** is a comfortable, centrally located inn near the South Rim of the canyon. (602) 638-2631.
- **Bright Angel Lodge,** the most lively spot to hang out, eat, etc., overlooks the Grand Canyon. (602) 638-2401.

FADE IN:
INTERIOR NEON—MORNING

The sun is rising bright as the cast leaves their rooms in the Kayenta Holiday Inn and sets out for Monument Valley, where they are scheduled to meet Navajo photojournalist Monty Roessel.

One of the many Navajo souvenir shanties that cater to tourists in Monument Valley.
SAM JONES

WADE: Check out that rock. That's cool.

BRAD: I think I saw that rock in a movie.

CHERI: What movie?

BRAD: I think it was that movie *The Searchers,* with Natalie Wood and John Wayne. That was a cool movie.

CHERI: So, when Indians live on reservations, are the rules the same? What's it like?

WADE: It's different for them. There are rules in there that don't apply out here.

BRAD: Like Billy Jack. You ever see that movie *Billy Jack*? People would be trying to mess with the Indians on the reservation ... he didn't play that.

WADE: Imagine being put on a reservation. I mean, they don't have to live there, but . . .

BRAD: Most of it's poorer than that town we just passed.

WADE: I know they get a certain amount of money from the government, but obviously it's not very much because they live very poor. There was one on "60 Minutes" one time that was just . . . literally like a ghetto. Crime and drugs and all that.

BRAD: And disease. Since they live so far

out, a lot of the plumbing and sewage isn't very good.

CHERI: Back in St. Louis, not far from us there are these Indian mounds that are pretty cool.

BRAD: I'd like to sit down and smoke a peace pipe with one of these suckers. You know, in one of those steam huts . . . see the spirits.

CUT TO:

EXTERIOR MONUMENT VALLEY—DAY

The group meets Monty Roessel, a Native American photojournalist who lives in the town of Kayenta in the Navajo Nation in Arizona.

They introduce themselves at the entrance to Monument Valley, which is lined on either side with a row of shanties, where Native Americans sell jewelry and trinkets.

CHERI: Do you live here?

MONTY: No, I live in Kayenta. It's about fifteen miles away, but I come out here a lot.

WADE: Do they make all this?

MONTY: Yeah. It's a federal law now, that if they're selling it, it has to say if it's made by Indians or if it's just a foreign trinket.

CHERI: Is this their full-time job? How they make a living?

MONTY: Not all these people make the jewelry. Other people will make it and sell it to these people and they sell it to the tourists. You see a lot of stores here because Kayenta and Monument Valley are such tourist traps. In other places, you'll see stores in more of a traditional, community setting.

WADE: Where do people live out here? I mean, when we were driving out here, I didn't see anything.

BRAD: I saw a school on the way.

MONTY: Yeah. In Kayenta, they have one of the nicest school systems in Arizona because there's a coal mine on top of the mesa there. So they have a tax base. They have a football field, two Olympic-size swimming pools; they have a grammar school, intermediate school, and high school; they have a gym that's bigger than most of the junior colleges'. The money comes in and they have to spend it somewhere, so they end up spending it on the school. The school's real nice. As you drive back, you'll see the real nice school, and across the street you'll see the BIA school. That's the federal school. Half of that's boarded up, wood over the windows, because they have no money, no tax base.

CHERI: Do you live on the reservation?

MONTY: Yeah, I live in Kayenta, but my home is in Round Rock. Most people, when they live out here, they have to work somewhere, so they might get a house near a school. But I'm from Round Rock, which is a very different community. It's very small. This little row of shacks is bigger than the whole town where I live. Navajos, you live where your mom lives. It's a matrilineal society, so you always consider that your home. That's where my home is.

CHERI: So you live in two places? I

Driving into Monument Valley was breathtaking. The clouds sat on the ground—it looked like an ocean with a huge wave coming in. When we drove into the cloud, visibility dropped to about 15 feet. You could barely see the car in front of you and it was about 15 to 20 degrees cooler. It was unreal!

thought you just either lived on the reservation or not.

MONTY: No. A lot of people think that it's some big deal, that you need a passport or something to come on the reservation. It's not like that. If you found a house for rent, like right over there, you could just rent it and move in without telling anybody. The problem is finding a place. You don't ever see houses for rent or apartments for rent. Most of the houses were built by a family and they keep that house or by the government or the school system. Schools get teachers from off the reservation—the majority of teachers are non-Navajo—so they need to find housing for them. The school will build all these houses for the teachers. It's not free, but almost. We have a four-bedroom house and it's only $175 a month. Even the BIA schools provide housing. I'm from Round Rock, but my wife teaches at the Kayenta school, so they provided a house for her. Once she quits her job, we no longer have a house.

WADE: I've seen stuff on TV about Indian reservations and it just seems like everything is run-down.

MONTY: Yeah. The appearance is sometimes confusing. The government sets the poverty level at "X" amount of dollars. But Navajos come from a culture that isn't based on dollars. So how can you judge their poverty? We have this and it doesn't look great, but why would you want to build something great here? Why would you want to build something permanent here? You can't compete with this and I'm only here for a couple of hours and then I go home. There are a lot of houses that look really run-down. That's the exterior, though. The peo-

Signs of traditional Native American life still survive in Monument Valley. The Navajos did not live in tepees but they have them here anyway. SAM JONES

ple are not like that. Sure you have people with their problems. But, like my family, we don't view it as a terrible thing. You can choose to leave if you want. The people who have the hardest time are the ones who leave and try to make it, but don't. A lot of them come back and they feel like a failure by somebody else's standards. Out here you're not judged like that.

WADE: Does anyone out here live well? I mean, is anyone rich?

MONTY: Again, it's a matter of perspective. As you drive through the reservation, you'll see some beautiful houses out there, but those houses are the result of something else. They're the result of a land dispute between the Hopi and the Navajo. The government had to relocate some people, so they would give them $55,000 or a house. So people have those houses sitting out there with no electricity and no running water.

WADE: They have no running water?

A Navajo peddler displays one of the cow skulls that he sells to tourists at Monument Valley. SAM JONES

MONTY: Well, the tribe tries to get water and electricity out there, but it's hard to justify. You have a priority list. If you have a hundred people on this road, and twelve that live over here, the hundred people will get services and the twelve will have to wait. Each pole costs so many thousands of dollars. So if you live a mile out, it will take so many poles and you can figure it out. You'll be like, "Gee, I think I'd rather have a generator in the back and use gasoline."

EILEEN: What kind of photography do you do?

MONTY: I was always upset when people would come in for a couple of weeks and photograph the culture and then leave and say,

"This is who the Navajo are." I photograph Indian life, mainly Navajo. Ceremonies . . . but when you think of ceremonies, people think you're trying to sensationalize, or it's a quick way to show the culture. I mean, when you think of Indians, you think of these clichés, that everything's run-down and everyone's running around in their headdresses. It's not like that. I try to break that myth down by showing everyday life, which does include ceremonies as well as kids going off to school, these kinds of places where people are selling jewelry, people making the jewelry . . . I try to show all parts of Navajo life that tell a story of who the Navajo are. One thing that I don't do, that's a major criticism of my work, is I don't photograph the problem with alcohol. I'll let the non-Navajos worry about that. I'm going to photograph what I think is the beauty of being a Navajo. If people want to see that part, they can see it, but I don't want to photograph it.

WADE: Why is it such a big problem?

MONTY: A lot of people have different reasons. I think it has a lot to do with making it in two different cultures. You'll be going through a border town and you'll just see rows of bars. Liquor is prohibited on the reservation. You can't drink it and you can't possess it. You'll see as you're coming in signs like, "Last chance for beer."

BRAD: Let me ask you something. This place looks real familiar. They use this in films?

MONTY: Yeah. Mel Gibson is coming in. He's doing a two-week shoot out here. I think it was John Ford who used to shoot a lot of westerns, old John Wayne movies out here.

BRAD: I told y'all that I saw this in a John Wayne movie!

MONTY: They're everywhere. They're the West. They're supposed to be the right mitten and the left mitten, the hands of Talking God, the holiest person of the Navajo.

WADE: How big is the reservation?

MONTY: The Navajo Nation is around twenty-three or twenty-five thousand square miles. It's about the size of West Virginia. It's huge.

WADE: Do the Navajo have any resentment toward white people . . . for putting them here and then coming in to just watch them?

MONTY: Yeah. You get a lot of that. Especially here because you have so many tourists coming through. But the Navajo are lucky in one way because the land that they're on is their traditional homeland. Other tribes, like the Cherokee, were moved and taken away from their homeland. In 1868, when the Navajo signed their treaty, the government came out here and looked around and said, "Who in hell would want to live out here?" And the Navajo raised their hands and said, "We do." And they keep growing. They buy a lot of land. If a ranch is for sale that borders the reservation, they buy it.

WADE: Where do they get that money?

MONTY: Like I said, the tribe has a coal mine, so we get royalties from the coal mine. Coming in through Utah, there's a lot of oil and natural gas, so they get royalties from that. At the same time, the tribe gets money from the federal government. When they signed the treaty, the government promised to take care of the Navajo with schools, education, roads, and things like that. So the tribe doesn't have to spend a lot of their money on those services. They make a lot of money. They have an operating budget of maybe a couple hundred million dollars.

WADE: Can't they use that money to build things up? Like water?

MONTY: They do, but again, you're looking at this area that's the size of West Virginia. In towns like Kayenta, you have water, electricity, phones, everything. But there are people who live way out and it takes a long time to get things out to them.

WADE: I don't think I could live out there.

MONTY: Again, though, it looks really run-down and that's the thing that probably strikes you when you come here. But the Navajo are not a people who are defined by what they live in or how they live. It's who they are and what they believe in. It's a very strong culture. It's probably the strongest culture of any Indian people who live in the country. Part of it is because of the land. When you come onto the reservation, you become the minority. The Navajo are always the vast majority here. You can't just swagger in and think you own the place. In the Navajo, there's a sense of family through the whole reservation.

EILEEN: Is it true that the Navajo language isn't written down anywhere?

MONTY: No, the Navajo language is a written language; it's very complex and detailed. In fact, during World War II, the Navajo language was used as a code and it's the only code in the history of war that's never been broken. Yet, at the same time, schools out here were trying to do what they called "scrub the Indian white." That was where they thought if they taught us English and took away our culture, we'd be just like them and they wouldn't need reservations. But that failed miserably. The Navajo didn't want to change. It shows some of that contradiction. They were using our language in war on the front lines while back here, kids were getting beaten and whipped for speaking their language in class.

CHERI: You said before that it's a matrilineal society.

MONTY: Navajos believe that the female is the most important.

EILEEN: That's a smart people.

MONTY: My wife says the same thing. Everything is traced back to the woman's side. While the man might go out and be the breadwinner, they're in charge of the home. And the home is very important. I'm not speaking of the home the way you might think of it. When you think of the home traditionally . . . there are four sacred mountains. There's a mountain in Colorado, Blanca Peak; there's one, Mount Taylor in New Mexico; San Francisco Peak, which you'll be driving by on the way to Flagstaff; and then there's one you can't see from here, La Plata, in the southwestern part of Colorado. That's what we consider the home. That's the round part of the home. Then you have two mountains in the middle and that's viewed as the doorway. The whole reservation is viewed as the home. So when the woman's in charge of the home, it's like she's in charge of everything that deals with the

Navajo photojournalist Monty Roessel stands before one of Monument Valley's "mittens." SAM JONES

home. Since everything has something to do with the home, they're in charge of everything.

EILEEN: Are they the ones who own the land, or is it equal?

MONTY: Well, Navajos don't believe in ownership. You can't own land. But, it will be equal, legally, as to who signs the lease or whatever. But that's just a formality. It doesn't mean anything to us, really.

CHERI: Do you ever feel like you want to live off the reservation?

MONTY: For me, I have kids. I want them to learn who they are and what it means to be a Navajo. It's important for them to know their history. You can't understand a culture going fifty-five miles an hour down the highway. You have to stop and meet people. So, like, last week I was down in Canyon de Chelly with this guy and just going through the canyon. He lives in the canyon. It's the only national park where people actually live within the boundaries. It's also very sacred to the Navajo. He was showing me all this stuff, like where a battle took place. I didn't know any of this. So now I can take my kids down there and they can know a little bit about it. But at the same time, I love it out there. Life is a lot slower. The clock slows down once you get out here. They joke about it being Indian time, but it's not just that. The time is more controlled by nature than by the second hand on a watch.

> When we ate lunch at a cafe, we all decided that our waitress was either an albino or possessed.

CUT TO:

INTERIOR NEON—AFTERNOON

Back on the road, the cast rolls on toward the Grand Canyon and a night beneath the stars.

CHERI: Is that the Grand Canyon?

WADE: Is it? No, that's just a shadow.

BRAD: You'll know when you're at the Grand Canyon.

CHERI: Have you been there before?

BRAD: No, but I've seen pictures of it. You'll know it. You don't see any cars or people, do you?

CHERI: Thank you, oh wise one. Seems like we're in the middle of nowhere.

WADE: It's just a great expanse.

BRAD: We're getting close.

CHERI: What are we gonna cook for dinner?

WADE: What do we have?

CHERI: We have S'mores, if Brad didn't eat all the chocolate.

BRAD: I ate all of it. I ate all the chocolate.

CHERI: So, ask us a question, Eileen.

Eileen picks up the *The Book of Questions* and thumbs through it.

EILEEN: All right. Let's see. Okay, this one's weird. For an all-expense-paid one-week vacation, would you be willing to kill a beautiful butterfly by pulling off his wings?

The Painted Desert looks like a fake backdrop in a movie. It's so beautiful that it doesn't look real.

CHERI: Of course!

EILEEN: How about stepping on a cockroach?

CHERI: We do that for fun.

BRAD: *(to Eileen)* Would you do it? Pull off a butterfly's wings?

Eileen doesn't answer.

CHERI: Is it one week?

WADE: I wouldn't care if it was a weekend. Who cares?

CHERI: You wouldn't do it?

WADE: I'd do it in a second.

BRAD: Wait, Eileen still didn't answer. Would you? Would you pull a butterfly's wings off?

CHERI: She's acting all righteous.

EILEEN: Not at all!

WADE: Are you serious?

CHERI: Eileen, you gotta figure that the next minute it might fly in front of a car and SMACK! There goes your vacation.

BRAD: She won't even answer!

EILEEN: No!

CHERI: What if you had to pull the wings off a butterfly to come on this trip?

BRAD: She would have jerked them off. She'd kill a damn animal. She'd shoot a cow.

EILEEN: That's dumb anyway.

As they round a bend, the Grand Canyon comes into view.

The cast soaks in the view from the Grand Canyon's South Rim, pondering Brad's conjecture that this gaping hole was the creation of prehistoric gophers. SAM JONES

BRAD: There it is! Look at that! That's a BIG hole.

WADE: That is. God! Look at that.

BRAD: Evel Knievel jumped over that.

WADE: He tried.

BRAD: He made it.

WADE: He did not!

BRAD: Did, too. He made it. He just crashed when he got to the other side.

WADE: If he did . . . the thing never made it to the other side. It ran right into the side, *smack!*

CHERI: Did he die?

BRAD: No, he lived.

WADE: He had this parachuted little rocket thing. I watched it on TV!

BRAD: I did, too. I could swear he made it across.

CHERI: I think I saw that.

WADE: He didn't make it across.

BRAD: Once he made it across. Maybe it was his son. Kevin Knievel? One of them jumped this Grand Canyon. It was on a motorcycle, too. He jumped right across this thing on a motorcycle. That's a big, long hole.

CHERI: It's enormous.

BRAD: All it is is a pathway where back in the dinosaur days a gigantic gopher used to crawl through. Prehistoric gopher. That's what that is.

WADE: Can you imagine how awesome it would be to go rafting through there and just look up and see how high it is?

BRAD: I'd like to base-jump off there. Man, it's gonna get cold out here tonight.

WADE: We'll have to put our tent somewhere where the wind is blocked.

BRAD: It's gonna be the most uncomfortable night's sleep so far.

WADE: It'll be fun.

CHERI: We'll just have to snuggle.

WADE: So we don't get hypothermia. All that rubbing up against each other. Grease ourselves up. . .

                                    CUT TO:

EXTERIOR CAMPGROUND—NIGHT

Our travelers pitch their tents and cook dinner.

EILEEN: I've been thinking about those congresspeople again.

WADE: Me, too.

They all laugh.

EILEEN: We know your views on that. But I just thought it was cool. I wish we could do it again. I've thought of a lot more things to ask them about.

BRAD: I thought it was interesting, listening to all their campaigning and B.S.

CHERI: That was not B.S. Pat Schroeder has been at the front of the women's-rights movement all these years. She's the one who took her kids to Capitol Hill to work because she couldn't afford a baby-sitter. She believes in what she does.

BRAD: She may believe in it, but that

Grand Canyon—even more breathtaking—climbed part way down—wow—one wrong step and that would be the end! Found our campsite—Wade and I set up the tents while Brad and Eileen went grocery shopping. Brad was really pissed.

doesn't dispute the fact that she was campaigning.

CHERI: That's your view.

BRAD: Every answer we got out there to every question was a drawn-out campaign speech. It wasn't an informal chat, it was an election-day speech. I'm not saying that they're not good people or they're not doing good things, but I'm saying they campaigned that day.

CHERI: I disagree. At least not with the women.

BRAD: Oh, the women didn't campaign? That's a sexist remark, right there.

CHERI: That's sexist? Okay, let's talk about sexist. Let's talk about sexism on this trip. Who can't go shopping? Who should do the cooking? When we were in the cabin, "Women, get in the kitchen."

BRAD: That has nothing to do with what you just said.

CHERI: Yes, it does. You brought up the topic of sexism and you are very sexist.

BRAD: No, we got on the topic of what you just said and that has no relevance. You said that the women weren't campaigning but the men were.

CHERI: That was a segue right into sexism.

BRAD: I have no comment on sexism. I'm not sexist and that's all I have to say about it.

CHERI: Didn't you say that the men should stay and set up the tents and the women should go shopping? That's what I heard. Didn't you guys have a discussion about this?

BRAD: I said it and I'll say it again. I still don't think I'm sexist. I'm not sexist at all.

CHERI: If that's not sexist, then what is?

BRAD: I just said I wanted to stay here and set up the tent.

CHERI: Why, because you feel like a pansy, going shopping?

BRAD: I don't go shopping. That's just the way I am.

CHERI: So, is a woman always going to shop for you?

BRAD: She might. I don't know. If it comes down to it, I'll go shopping, but I'd rather not. I'd rather sit right here and fix the tent. And you, being a female, I would have thought that you would have enjoyed going shopping instead.

CHERI: Me as a female because I love grocery shopping!

BRAD: Rather than fix the tent.

EILEEN: If I knew how to set up a tent, I'd be there in a second. That is definitely sexist.

BRAD: I was trying to be considerate. It had nothing to do with sexism at all.

CHERI: Wait. You had a little hissy fit because the guy is supposed to set up the tent. Then you said, "I'm not going to shop at all. I'm just going to stand there."

BRAD: Did I go shopping?

EILEEN: Well, I put him in his place. I think he's progressing.

BRAD: Put him in his place? See, that's a sexist remark right there.

EILEEN: Well, when you act like that, you get it back.

BRAD: You don't understand my viewpoint.

CHERI: Well, tell us. We want to understand.

BRAD: It's like working on a car. If we were sitting around the house and somebody was already in the garden, planting flowers or something . . .

EILEEN AND CHERI: You are digging a *hole!*

BRAD: No, check this out. If me and someone were out there working on a car, you walk out and you're like, "I'm so bored. I want something to do." I would probably suggest that you go and work in the flowerbed.

CHERI: What do you think Wade would rather do?

WADE: For the most part you have to admit that. . .

EILEEN: For the most part, you can't generalize like that. Maybe I have a thing for cars and I would much rather work with you.

WADE: Do you believe in equality all the way around?

No response.

WADE: You have to believe in all or nothing. Do you believe in it all the way around or not?

EILEEN: I do.

CHERI: Then you're going to say that women should be drafted.

WADE: Yeah.

CHERI: Well, they should draft them but maybe not put them on the front line.

BRAD: Oh, yes. You should have to fight and get killed just like everybody else.

CHERI: They should get positions they can handle physically.

BRAD: But if a woman can't handle what a man can, then she shouldn't be treated equally. If you should have equal treatment in one aspect, you should have equal treatment in all. If you want to be treated like a man . . .

CHERI: I don't want to be treated like a man. I want to be treated equal. There are certain physical things that I can't do.

BRAD: Then I would assume that you would want to work in the flowerbed rather than work on the car because there are certain physical things that you can't do. Like you might not be strong enough to turn that bolt down there on the engine.

CHERI: There's a difference between putting a tent up and having to change an engine. We're talking apples and oranges here, so why are you bringing it up?

BRAD: Well, you're the exception. Most girls would not know how to put a tent up.

CHERI: So I rode the bike the other day. Would most girls do that? Maybe not.

BRAD: That's what I'm saying.

CHERI: But you know me. And all of a sudden you categorize me as a woman and instantly this is what she'd want to do. You just assume that I'm a woman, therefore I should be shopping.

BRAD: I'm just saying that the majority of

> Brad was pissed that we woke Wade up because he started farting again. I don't know how Brad could breathe in that gas-filled tent.

women would not know how to put the tent up
and would have gone shopping. I mean, for
real, do you think the majority of women
that you know would have wanted to put the
tent up more than go shopping?

EILEEN: I know tons of girls who are out-
doorsy and would love to stay and put up the
tent.

BRAD: I didn't say tons. I said the majority of women that you know.

CHERI: The people I hang around with would
have been glad to stay here and put up the
tent. All you have to do is follow directions.

BRAD: Be honest. Just be honest.

EILEEN: I help my dad with a lot of stuff.

BRAD: That's not what I asked. All you
have to do is say yes or no. And be honest
about it. Say yes or no and the discussion
will be over. Say yes and I guess I was
wrong and y'all are right.

CHERI: Then yes.

EILEEN: Yes.

BRAD: All right. You can lie to me, but
don't lie to yourself.

FADE OUT.

DAY 18:

TRAVEL: 275 miles/ 5.5 hours raw drive time.

You get one hour, absolutely free. When you cross the Hoover Dam into Nevada you're on Pacific Time.

PLACES OF INTEREST:
- **The Meteor Museum.** Although it's forty miles east of Flagstaff, it might be worth a look. Take a gander at this mile-wide hole in the ground, created by a fallen meteor. Afterward, check out the **Astronaut Hall of Fame,** located in the adjacent **Museum of Astrogeology.** Just off I-40 at Exit 233. (602)774-8350.
- Get your kicks . . . turn off I-40 at Seligman for a loop across a section of **Old Route 66.** You'll know you're there. Towns along the way boast of being part of the highway culture at every opportunity.
- **The Hoover Dam** plugs up the Colorado River and delivers you into Nevada. It's worthwhile to stop and take a closer look at this amazing feat of engineering.

NIGHTLIFE:
- Just about the only thing to do at night in Vegas is gamble. Although the Strip is home to more theme-park-oriented casinos, gamblers in the know prefer the downtown section on Fremont Street and casinos such as **The Horseshoe,** home of the World Series of Poker and single-deck blackjack.

ACCOMMODATIONS:
- **Motel 6.** This one actually has a neon sign. 195 East Tropicana Boulevard, Las Vegas. (702)798-0728.

FADE IN:
INTERIOR NEON—MORNING.

After getting up early to watch the sun rise over the Grand Canyon, the cast packs up and rolls ever west toward Las Vegas.

WADE: I think we should wear our cowboy hats in Vegas. It's gonna be about the only chance we have to wear them on this trip.

BRAD: There's no cowboys in Vegas.

WADE: Christ, there's every walk of life in Vegas.

BRAD: There's only mobsters in Vegas.

WADE: That's the only thing you don't see. You don't see those kind. You'll see a lot of dudes in cowboy hats, high-roller dudes with dough. They'll be sitting at the tables . . . the best thing to do is go into a place like Caesar's Palace and just watch everything that's going on. You'll see people just throwing away the cash. Just thousands of dollars, like it's nothing.

CHERI: Maybe Eileen and I will get some rich guy to toss us some cash so we can gamble.

BRAD: You probably will. I'm gonna go in there and put on western wear. I'll put on a black suit and my cowboy hat and get down with some rich woman that's gonna take care of me.

WADE: What are you doing back there?

BRAD: This Band-Aid on my leg is stuck into my hair.

WADE: Just whip it quick, dude!

CHERI: That's what you're whining about

We discovered microphones on our tents. I don't think they have anything really incriminating, but if they took clips of our conversations, they could make us look pretty bad.

Packing up their tent before hitting the road to Vegas. SAM JONES

back there? You're worried about being a man and you can't pull a Band-Aid off your leg? I'd rather a guy cry about something that really affects him emotionally than whimper about pulling a Band-Aid off.

BRAD: Let me alone. I'll do it when I'm ready.

WADE: I gotta get a mountain bike. That was so cool. My mom would be like, "You don't have to spend your money on that!" But I could do that every weekend. I'd much rather do that than go out. I'm getting to that point where I've gone out enough.

CHERI: Me too.

BRAD: Man, I've got to fart. I've been trying to hold it in, but it's been cramping up my stomach for the past hour.

CHERI: Why don't you just let it go?

BRAD: I can't get it out, now!

WADE: Last night I couldn't even stop if I had to. Every thirty seconds I was like, *braaap, braaap.* Woke up this morning . . .

CHERI: And your hair was green?

WADE: Usually if they're loud, they're not bad.

BRAD: That's right. It's when they're quiet that they get you.

WADE: These were bad, though. I was fanning the covers and it went clear over to Brad's bed.

CHERI: I'm glad you weren't in my tent.

WADE: I'm bored. *Heeere* pig pig pig pig pig. You ever hear a hog calling contest? Souie! Souie! *Heeeere* pig pig pig pig pig pig pig pig! *Souuuuuie! Souuuuuie!*

In 1984, the bypassing of historic Route 66 was completed. The demise of the romantic road spelled trouble for towns that once served as pit stops for cross-country travelers. Brad is interviewed at one of the many abandoned gas stations along the Mother Road, this one in Seligman, AZ. SAM JONES

CHERI: I'm impressed.

WADE: I like to do that on first dates, when I really want them to like me. Remember that song, "My Sharona"? I can do that with my nose.

He sniffs out the tune to "My Sharona."

WADE: You just gotta make sure you don't blow boogs out when you do that. My Sharona!

BRAD: Who did that song?

WADE: Wasn't that Styx? Or, no, it was that band The Knack. Get The Knack.

BRAD: I always liked that band The Thompson Twins.

WADE: I still like them. "Hold Me Now"? "Lies, Lies, Lies"?

BRAD: And that other guy, Thomas Dolby?

WADE AND CHERI: "She Blinded Me with Science!"

WADE: Good heavens, Miss Mergatroid, You're beautiful!

BRAD: Man, this is killing me.

CHERI: Are you still playing with that Band-Aid? You wuss! Eileen, do it for him.

BRAD: Okay, just let me close my eyes. Do it fast.

CHERI: No, Eileen, do it really slow.

BRAD: Fast, fast!

CHERI: Slow!

EILEEN: Brad, just chill out. Here we go.

BRAD: *Ooooooowwwch!*

WADE: She didn't even get it!

They laugh.

BRAD: She left it halfway on!

WADE: Give it to me. I'll get that thing off there in a heartbeat.

He reaches into the back seat and RIPS the Band-Aid off.

BRAD: *Aaaahhhh!*

EILEEN: Ouch.

WADE: Look at that thing. He said it was deep. It's a strawberry! He was barely scraped.

BRAD: It was bleeding. I damn near bled to death.

CHERI: I've never heard someone cry so much about skinning their knee.

WADE: I am so amped to get to Vegas.

BRAD: I'm tired. I'm just gonna go to sleep.

WADE: Bullshit. You're not going to bed. There's so much to see you won't want to go to sleep.

EILEEN: Okay, everybody go to sleep now. You, too, Wade.

BRAD: Man, I hate that, when I'm driving at night and the rest of y'all go to sleep. Y'all are bastards.

CHERI: Who's ever stayed awake when I drive?

BRAD: You never drive at night.

CHERI: I'm so tired. If I don't get some shuteye, I'm going to be dead tomorrow.

EILEEN: What are we doing tomorrow?

CHERI: Rock climbing.

EILEEN: Sweet.

CHERI: What are you drinking up there, Brad?

BRAD: Crow's piss.

CHERI: Can I have some?

Brad hands her a drink.

WADE: Man, what if one of us really hits it big tonight? Like a million-dollar jackpot?

BRAD: I'll say, "Bye! Have a nice life, y'all."

CHERI: You wouldn't even share?

BRAD: With you? Get real, woman.

WADE: I could definitely use some cash.

CHERI: I would quit work and just travel all over the place.

EILEEN: I would finish school, then travel.

BRAD: I would settle down, buy some land . . .

WADE: I would still work. I'd go nuts just sitting around all the time. The job I'm going to do, I know I'm not going to make a lot of money, but it's something I know I want to do.

CHERI: I love money.

WADE: I think it's different for women than it is for men. Women can always marry someone who has money. They can always take

I didn't want to say anything that I would regret and the thoughts I was having were truly harmful. Lashing out would only create more animosity.

a job doing whatever and know that they can marry someone that has cash.

EILEEN: I don't know. I think that's old hat.

WADE: Eileen, you think everything is from the past and it's not. Women still look at men for money. It might be sexist, but that's the way it is.

CHERI: I know what you're saying. Sometimes I get nervous about the situation I'm in. I've had my degree for several years now and I haven't had a job for a while. Sometimes I think, "Yeah I could just marry a rich man." But I don't want to have to depend on someone else.

EILEEN: I think someone has to have pretty low self-esteem just to marry someone for their money.

WADE: But the opportunity is still there.

CHERI: I haven't dated many rich guys and I don't think the odds are very good that I'll marry one. It would be one more worry in my life to have to find a rich man. What happens if you get married and things go bad? I don't want to end up on welfare. I want to be able to support myself no matter what.

EILEEN: You're right, Wade, that a woman has a better opportunity to marry someone rich, but that's because it's a male-dominated world. A man gets paid a dollar to a woman's eighty cents. Look at this, there's a new female condom out and it costs three times as much as a male condom. And women make less money. And I think women who marry for money have low self-esteem and that's it.

BRAD: Hold on now. If you would be honest here, I mean totally honest . . . Okay, if two guys liked y'all, say y'all are dating two guys each, and both guys are nice and both guys are good-looking. One guy doesn't make much money. He makes $20,000 a year. The other guy is an executive for IBM and he makes $200,000 a year. Both of them like you a lot. Which one are you going to want to marry?

WADE: They're going to say it depends on their personality.

BRAD: But they know damn well which one they want to marry.

EILEEN: You think we're so shallow and materialistic.

BRAD: Y'all are not being honest.

CHERI: No, wait a minute. I was dating this guy with a lot of money. He drove a Stealth and was really cool. And it was fun riding around in a Stealth. It's exciting and you can do more things with him.

BRAD: See, exactly.

CHERI: But once you get further into the relationship and you find out about them as a person, you may not like it. Maybe they're so driven by money that that's really all that's important to him. You'll just say one day, "What is this?" And you have to live with it every day of your life.

BRAD: Come on now. If you went to a bar and you met a guy and you're smiling at him and he's smiling at you, and he looks real good, and you both walked outside and he got into a damn lime-green pinto with the muffler hanging down . . . and then you went back into the bar and saw another guy and y'all eyeing each other, and he walked out and got into a new 500SL Mercedes, which guy are you gonna give your phone number?

CHERI: I've never known anyone to ask a guy what kind of car he drives before going out on a date or sees him drive up and go, "Oh, no." If he drives up in a Corvette, you're like, "Whoa!" It's just an added bonus. I'll tell you, if a guy tries to impress me by throwing out what kind of car he has in casual conversation, I won't give him the time of day.

EILEEN: Why are we arguing about this?

BRAD: Arguing? This isn't arguing. This is discussing. I ain't arguing with anybody.

CHERI: Okay, here's a question for you. Out of me and Eileen, who do you think will find the rich guy?

WADE: Cheri.

BRAD: Eileen.

EILEEN: Why me? How can you say that?

BRAD: Just because that's who you'll be around most of your life. You do all that jet-setting and traveling, and once you get out of college, you're gonna be surrounded by rich guys and that's who you're gonna marry.

CHERI: Why me?

WADE: Just because of your personality. She's set against it and says no and you've already said that money excites you.

CHERI: What kind of woman do you think you guys will marry?

EILEEN: Brad will marry someone sub-servient. Someone who does all the cooking and cleaning for him.

I put Brad in his place, telling him that when I am having a serious conversation with someone that he should keep quiet—no laughing, mocking, making fun, etc. Sometimes his 3rd grade mentality drives me nuts.

BRAD: It's insulting to say that they would be subservient. All the girls I go out with are very strong women. They argue with me just like y'all do.

CHERI: What kind of guy will Eileen marry?

WADE: Someone very conservative, suit-and-tie. Someone very traditional, very disciplined. Someone who doesn't mind eating the same meal all the time. Not someone who's flashy or a risk-taker. How about Cheri?

BRAD: I think Cheri's man will be just the opposite. I think he'll be wild and loud and adventurous.

WADE: I don't. I think he'll have to be very tolerant and he'll have to be subservient to her. He's going to have to be very patient. Someone who likes to do things, but very patient and laid back.

CHERI: My dad's real laid back. I can see myself marrying someone like that.

BRAD: Check that out! Out on the right there! That's the place they shot that film *Universal Soldier*. You ever see that?

WADE: What is that?

BRAD: Hoover Dam. That's where they shot that movie. Dolf Lundgren and Jean-Claude Van Damme. Bad movie.

WADE: Almost in Vegas.

CHERI: Last time I went gambling I won.

WADE: I usually don't gamble. I know how long it takes to earn my money and I just get pissed off when I see it go like that.

BRAD: I'm not a gambling man, myself. I'd rather put my money on something I have control over. It's one thing to put money on a basketball game if I'm playing because I know it's up to me to win.

WADE: Check this out. In Vegas they do all these things to keep you gambling. When you get there you'll see it. First of all, they pump oxygen into the casinos. They pump pure oxygen in so you don't get tired at the tables. And when you're sitting there gambling they give you free drinks. As long as you keep gambling they give you all the cocktails you want. And then there aren't any windows. You can't see outside while you're gambling. It's amazing. You can just lose all track of time. Food's really cheap, too. You can eat for nothing.

BRAD: I'd like to see some Mafia heads.

WADE: It's kind of amazing to think that it's all really run that way, like you see in the movies.

BRAD: The thing about the Mafia, though, is that it's actually more organized than this country. I have this friend, Jonathan, who actually feels that this country would be a lot better off if the Mafia ran it.

CHERI: Wellll . . .

EILEEN: They're organized, but they're violent.

BRAD: But there's corruption in our government now.

CHERI: But they'll just go, "We don't like this family so we're going to bomb them."

WADE: But there's a lot of respect between families. You don't see that very often. That's why, for the most part, they're very respectful. They know that, "If I do him,

Where else but Las Vegas would be home to the Liberace Museum, where one might stroll the gallery of the maestro's understated performance wardrobe?
COURTESY OF LIBERACE MUSEUM

he's gonna do me . . . " and that kind of thing.

BRAD: I think the Mafia's cool. If I were Italian, I'd be in it. I swear I would. If I had the chance I would most definitely be in it. The way they run things, I'd rather work for them than probably anybody.

CHERI: Like as a hit man?

BRAD: No, I'd want to be able to be the man one day.

EILEEN: You don't understand how precious life is.

BRAD: Yes, I do. I didn't say I wanted to be a hit man. Cheri said that.

EILEEN: Because of your whole spiel, yesterday. They're totally violent. It's just wrong.

BRAD: Who's the governor of New York?

EILEEN: Cuomo. Mario Cuomo.

BRAD: There.

WADE: What's your point?

BRAD: Look what he's done to New York. He hasn't done that, the Mafia's done that. Cuomo, I'm telling you, if he ran for president, I'd vote for him. Simply because he's connected to the Mafia.

EILEEN: I really wonder where you get this stuff, Brad.

CHERI: *(to Wade)* Why did you say before that somebody would need patience with me? I mean, I can see your point sometimes, but I think I just voice my opinion. Sometimes I am kind of picky, but I'm just particular.

WADE: I don't think you're particular at all. I think you have to be right so you say it and say it until a person's just like, "Fine, take it, whatever." Like the other day you wanted something and you just said it like six times. You said it once and we heard you, but you had to keep saying it until it's just like, "Okay already, do it." Or it's like the other night when you said I keep to myself and don't say anything. Then I go off and you get upset.

CHERI: You got all upset that I said that. One simple thing. It was like a major insult to you. To me, you just sit there and analyze things and keep things to yourself. I didn't say that was bad or good. I was just making a comment. Apparently it really offended you because you got really upset about it.

WADE: Because when I hear people say something that's just totally off, I say something about it. But I don't like to argue back and forth about it. I say something once and I've said what I have to say about it. You'll end up perpetuating and keeping it going. That's what bugs me. Every remark that's said, you have something to say back and it's just like, "Jesus, leave it alone." Can anyone ever say anything without you popping in and saying something back about it? At first you don't notice things like that. You don't know someone and you're tolerant about it. Then as time goes on, I pick up this pattern and see how it is. That's why my patience has been real short.

EILEEN: Look at all those lights. That's amazing.

WADE: It's not that I dislike you. It's

just one of the things that you do that gets on my nerves. We can go through ninety percent of the day and everything's fine. But there's that ten percent where you do that and I'll just be like, "God."

EILEEN: I don't think my husband will be that boring. I want someone with a sense of humor.

WADE: This car is just filled with excitement. I don't know why you're taking it so personally. You want me to say stuff and when I do you don't say shit back.

CHERI: I'm just thinking about it. I'm not going to change your mind, so why should I try?

WADE: So now you understand why I just sit back and let you guys argue.

CHERI: When Brad and I argue I'm not trying to change Brad's mind and he's not trying to change mine. We're just discussing our viewpoints. This is just something that you feel one way about and I feel another way about. Just like with the tent. I thought the tag should go in the front. That was logical. So you didn't see it that way. So we spend all this time trying to figure out how it goes and the tag ends up on the front. What was I to say? Or it's like the credit card sign. How could they take it from in state, but not out of state? That made no sense to me.

WADE: Because it said NO CREDIT CARDS! You piss me off so much!

CHERI: I had to bring that up because you were asking.

WADE: SHUT UP!

CHERI: See, why should I bring it up?

WADE: Because you act like an idiot!
That's why. You want to know why I don't
like to get pissed off? Because I get ruth-
less and I don't like to be like that. You
are always right.

CHERI: No I'm not.

WADE: Bullshit. Last night when we were
having that discussion about sexism, you
were looking at Brad with such vengeance in
your eyes. I was looking at you and I was
getting pissed off because you just wanted
to drill it right down his throat. You were
like, "How moronic can you be?" I just
thought, "What a bitch."

CHERI: All right, maybe I was a bitch
about that. But it's something I had to
deal with. Just like he gets really hyped
about racial things.

BRAD: I never attacked any one of y'all
about that. I just discussed and got your
viewpoints and let you know mine. But last
night both of you did attack me. It's all
right, though.

EILEEN: I just want to enjoy the lights.

BRAD: But you both got what you wanted
because I admitted I was wrong. You both
got what you wanted.

EILEEN: Don't start with me, Brad.

BRAD: You wouldn't be getting offended at
me right now if you didn't know I was right.

EILEEN: You always have to be right.

BRAD: I always have to be right, but you
still attacked me last night. That's all
I'm saying. I was trying to talk in a
rational tone and you attacked me. And you
know it.

WADE: You were just trying to make him look stupid.

CHERI: Well, he got to the point where he wasn't even making sense.

BRAD: I was making sense.

WADE: Just think if I said this two days into the trip. We'd have had a blast. Lucky we only have two left.

BRAD: All I was saying there was that most girls that I know would rather go shopping than to stay in the woods and put up a tent. And I didn't mean it to be sexist.

EILEEN: You just think it's an attack every time you don't win.

BRAD: I still won. Y'all tried to make me look bad and I didn't.

CHERI: It's happened this whole trip, all these remarks like, "Why don't you girls get in there and cook me up some dinner?" You say it as a joke, but it gets old. It's not cute. We're trying to have a conversation about it and all you do is sit there and laugh.

BRAD: I can laugh if I want to. How come I can't laugh?

CHERI: Because we're trying to have a conversation and trying to deal with it.

BRAD: So now you're trying to have a rational conversation.

CHERI: We're sorry we attacked you last night. It's just been building to a head the whole trip and we just started feeding off of each other and that's what happened. We got upset.

EILEEN: Maybe you shouldn't have said anything to me.

BRAD: I'm not sexist. I am not sexist. The whole remark was not sexist.

WADE: This world is sexist. You can't expect people to never say things or never have attitudes that are that way.

CHERI: Just like this world is racist.

BRAD: Did I jump on you? I just try to tell you how I think about it, but you jumped on me. I never jumped on you.

CHERI: It's frustrating. Those racist things are frustrating to you and sexist things are frustrating to us.

BRAD: But it's how you handle it that makes all the difference.

EILEEN: But you jumped down Cheri's throat after the Civil Rights Museum when she said she wouldn't pick up an African history book.

BRAD: I did not jump down her throat.

CHERI: Yes you did, Brad.

WADE: The whole thing about an argument is that nobody wins.

They drive in silence through the bright lights of Vegas to their hotel.

                                    CUT TO:

INTERIOR NEON—NIGHT

No one can stay mad too long in Vegas. Having put their differences aside, the cast spends the night cruising the Strip and gambling.

It's still dark, but dawn approaches as the Neon carries them back to their motel.

WADE: I wish I was a math wizard.

CHERI: So you could count cards?

WADE: Yeah. But some guys like that are only allowed to win a certain amount. I was listening to this guy on the radio a while back and he's got this math book that's out about making math easier, stuff they don't show you at school. He can come to Vegas and win six grand, guaranteed, every time he comes, but that's the limit that they'll let him take. There are certain guys they know, geniuses who can do that. And if they know you can do it, then you're limited. But he could go to a casino and just cash in.

CHERI: So why doesn't he do that all the time?

WADE: I guess he's making all this money elsewhere. He's making it on this book. But I'm sure he's got to come down here. I mean, you want to make a hundred grand you just come down here for a couple of weeks.

CHERI: But don't they label you?

WADE: That's what I mean, he's labeled. They know when he's there.

BRAD: For some reason I just got tired.

WADE: I'll tell you why you got tired. It's because in the casino they were pumping in oxygen.

CHERI: Is that really it?

BRAD: It's got to be, 'cause the minute I got in this car I was dead tired. I can barely keep my eyes open right now.

WADE: Look at that . . . pawn shops everywhere. This is the place to go to find some good stuff. People just hock everything to get cash.

CHERI: That's the job to have, working at a casino.

WADE: Why?

CHERI: Whenever people win money, they tip you.

WADE: You work long hours, though. You're not making much as an hourly wage.

CHERI: Well, not for a lifetime job, but just for some cash. It's like a Disneyland for adults.

FADE OUT.

DAY 19:

Thursday, October 14:

Las Vegas, NV, to Los Angeles, CA

TRAVEL: 275 miles/5.5 hours raw drive time

PLACES OF INTEREST:
- **Liberace Museum.** The rings, the costumes, the pianos, the candelabras—they're all here, in living color. 1775 East Tropicana Avenue, Las Vegas. (702)798-5595.
- **The Survival Store.** Thought guns were only for boys? Think again. Ask Bo (a former *Penthouse* pet) for some target practice. 3250 Pollux Avenue, Las Vegas. (702)871-7795.
- **Whiskey Pete's** will just about be your last chance to gamble as you cruise toward L.A. on I-15. It's also home to Bonnie and Clyde's actual death car.

→ **RED ROCKS** is one of the finest sites for rock climbing in the Southwest. Stop in at **Desert Rock Sports** and get outfitted for a half-day climb just outside Vegas. 7034 West Charleston Avenue, Las Vegas. (702)254-1143.

PLACES TO EAT:
- **The Green Shack** is a great place to escape the glaring neon of Vegas and enjoy some country cooking here. 2504 Fremont Street. (702)383-0007.
- **Peggy Sue's Diner** is a '50s time warp just off I-15 in Yermo, California. (619)254-3370.

NIGHTLIFE:
Los Angeles:
- **The Sunset Strip,** on Sunset Boulevard, between La Cienega and Robertson, is home to the rock-and-roll venues that defined L.A. music from The Doors to Guns 'n Roses. Check out **The Roxy, The Whiskey A Go Go, Gazzari's,** and the latest addition, Johnny Depp's **Viper Room.**

- If you prefer a more laid-back scene, catch the jazz stylings of Marty and Elayne Roberts, an act transplanted straight from a Vegas lounge into **The Dresden Room,** at 1760 North Vermont Avenue. (213) 665-4294.
- The coffeehouse scene is burgeoning in Hollywood. A prime example is **Highland Grounds,** where they serve up java and live music. 742 North Highland Avenue. (213)466-1507.
- **McCabe's Guitar Shop** in Santa Monica is renowned not only for its instruments, but as a venue for great acoustic music. 3101 Pico Boulevard. (310) 828-4497.
- If you venture downtown, check out **Al's Bar.** It's a divy host to alternative music and an arty clientele. 305 South Hewitt Street. (213)687-3558.

ACCOMMODATIONS:
- **The Chateau Marmont** is convenient to the Sunset Strip and is probably most famous for being the death site of John Belushi. 8211 West Sunset Boulevard. (213)656-1010.
- **Motel 6,** 5101 West Century Boulevard. (310) 419-1234.

FADE IN:
INTERIOR NEON—DAY

Our travelers wake up tired but excited as they grab breakfast and pile into the car for the drive to the Red Rocks, outside Vegas, where they will try their hands at rock climbing.

BRAD: I bet their power bills are high here. I bet Nevada Power is having a field day here.

WADE: All this electricity. . .

BRAD: They must make a hell of a lot of money on gambling. I was trying to guess how much they had to pay in that film *Indecent Proposal* to rent that casino out. I bet it cost a million dollars.

> Rock climbing was on our agenda. Massive walls surrounded us and when you looked closely, you could see tiny objects moving on the cliffs. Those were climbers. We couldn't believe it.

Eileen conquers her fear of heights on the face of a rock at Red Rocks, just outside of Las Vegas. SAM JONES

Daredevil cameraman Jonathan Rho will do just about anything to get the shot. SAM JONES

Brad probably had the most difficulty climbing. At one point, he yelled down that he was scared. That made me feel great, not that he was scared, but that he admitted it. He seemed to change the most, to grow the most during the trip.

CHERI: Look at that woman's butt. Big old butt.

BRAD: I didn't see her. Where? Oh, my God.

WADE: Why would you wear something like that? Look at the dimples in her legs.

BRAD: They're like caverns. They're like the Grand Canyon in there.

WADE: There should be a picture of that on every girl's refrigerator.

BRAD: Just to remind them.

CHERI: So many people out here are fat.

BRAD: I know. I kept expecting to see these beautiful people and high rollers. It's all just regular people.

CHERI: Regular fat people.

BRAD: Everybody's all pale . . . they didn't look so happy, either.

WADE: There was that one guy, the one playing craps. We couldn't play because he was running the table. They couldn't close him down because he'd won so much money. They wanted him to keep going so he'd lose some back.

CHERI: How much did he win?

WADE: I heard someone say that he was up by $15,000 at one point.

BRAD: Yeah, he must have been up by a lot because I saw him at the cashier and he was just smiling away.

WADE: Who won the most money last night?

CHERI: I won about $150.

WADE: Did anybody lose?

CHERI: Eileen.

EILEEN: Not too much.

CHERI: How did you do, Wade?

WADE: I guess I broke even.

EILEEN: This town looks so much better at night.

WADE: Yeah, it really loses it during the day.

                                    CUT TO:

INTERIOR NEON—AFTERNOON

Tired but pumped from their success on the rocks, they set off for the final leg of their journey, the road to Los Angeles.

EILEEN: *(to Cheri)* What are you reading back there?

CHERI: Oh, Joey Buttafuocco finally admitted he had an affair with that girl.

EILEEN: Who? Amy Fisher?

BRAD: He still didn't tell her to kill his wife, regardless.

CHERI: She's still standing by him even though she said that if she found out he was involved she'd cut his testicles off.

EILEEN: That's sick. Speaking of mutilation, Brad, you don't have much of a chance left to get your tattoo.

BRAD: I'm getting it in Los Angeles.

EILEEN: Where are you going to get it?

BRAD: I'm gonna get it at this famous place . . . I'm not sure where it is.

EILEEN: No, I mean, are you going to get it on your back?

Brad decided to get a tattoo, but almost wimped out at the last minute. He had been talking about getting one the whole trip, but I think he would have been relieved if it didn't work out. He chose a tiger print. I've never seen a person get a tattoo—strange—it looks like the artist is simply drawing on your skin, but from the look on Brad's face we knew this wasn't the case.

"This won't hurt a bit." Brad gets his tattoo at Easyriders on Melrose Avenue. SAM JONES

BRAD: Oh, yeah.

EILEEN: Are you going to get the dragon?

BRAD: Dragon or tiger. I'm not sure. I've always wanted to get one or the other, but if I get a dragon, I'll catch hell in my tae kwon do class.

EILEEN: Why?

BRAD: Because, each art has an animal that it represents and the tiger represents tae kwon do. And my instructor is big into that.

WADE: So what if, before you had taken the class, you had a tattoo of Porky Pig on your ass?

BRAD: I know. There's a dude that comes in that has a dragon on his arm. He's got to cover it up. Even under his uniform, he's got to tape it up.

CHERI: I can't wait to get to L.A.

BRAD: I want to get back home.

EILEEN: How come?

BRAD: I just feel like my whole life is on hold. We've only been gone for three weeks, but it feels like I've been gone for three months.

EILEEN: Yeah, we've done a lot in three weeks.

BRAD: I just can't wait to get back to my life. Even though I didn't want it to happen, I guess I changed a lot more than I thought I was gonna.

EILEEN: In what way?

BRAD: Just done a lot of changing. More than you know.

EILEEN: It's definitely been an experience.

BRAD: You're gonna go back to Boston and your friends won't even know you, you'll be acting so different.

EILEEN: Why? I'm the same person.

BRAD: You're gonna go back and say stuff like, "I gotta piss like a nine-dick weasel."

EILEEN: That's about as funny as a church fire.

CHERI: To me it's not that big of a deal. St. Louis will always be there. I'm not in that big of a hurry.

BRAD: I like being me. I want to get back to where I like being me at. I love Atlanta.

CHERI: I like where I live, but I like a change of pace. I love to vacation.

WADE: This was no vacation, this was work.

CHERI: It was a vacation to me. I love to vacation. I might go to Brazil this winter.

BRAD: I don't like traveling that much. I loved doing this trip so I could say I've been to all these places. But as far as traveling, I don't really care for it.

CHERI: Man, the best time in my life was backpacking in Europe. I remember every detail of that trip. I'll always think of that as the most amazing thing.

BRAD: The simple stuff entertains me. I have fun just standing around and shooting pool with my friends. I just have the best times in my life doing things like that; shooting pool, going to a movie with my girlfriend, stuff like that. I'll just sit there by myself watching old westerns on the couch.

WADE: I'll be glad to get back to Oregon. I loved growing up there. When I was younger, we used to have these chases on dirt bikes, these little motorcycles. We'd chase each other all over the place. It was nuts. I still have a scar on my knee from that.

BRAD: I have a huge burn scar on my leg from crashing a motorcycle when I was a kid. The muffler part fell on my leg right here. I'll never forget it. I thought my dad was gonna kill me. I went over to this guy's house and my dad told me not to get on the boy's motorcycle. He had these dirt mounds in the back of his house and we were riding around there and I wrecked it. Burned myself real bad right there on my leg. The skin was just hangin' off.

EILEEN: Oh, nice image!

BRAD: I was hurtin' bad, but I didn't want to tell his mom, because I knew she would tell my dad. I didn't tell anybody. It was the middle of summer. I had shorts on when it happened, but I started wearing blue jeans in the middle of summer. That's the reason I got caught. It was like July or August and everyone was like, "Why are you wearing blue jeans?" I would just be like, "'Cause I want to." And I would walk funny because it hurt so much. I went that way for a week with skin hanging off and walking all funny. Then I went over to my grandma's house and I was walking like that and my uncle Bob was like, "Boy, why are you walking like that? You're walking like you got a corn cob stuck up your butt." And all my uncles got in on it and then my dad got in on it. He was like, "Why you got those jeans on? Somethin' wrong with you, boy?" He came and patted me down and, *bam!* Right on the burn. I screamed. He took me into the bathroom and it was like this close to getting infected.

WADE: You gotta cover it.

BRAD: I hadn't done anything. And you know how you get cotton and lint and everything from your jeans, that was all stuck in there. They took me to a doctor.

CHERI: Did they have to peel it?

BRAD: They peeled it and washed it . . . it hurt so bad. And my dad was probably madder that I didn't tell him than if I'd gone ahead and told him.

EILEEN: We have a pool in our backyard and kids would come at night all the time. We'd find cigarettes and cigarette burns on the deck and all . . . sometimes we'd hear them but they'd . . .

BRAD: They'd swim in your own pool and you wouldn't know it?

CHERI: Sure. They'd go pool hopping.

BRAD: People would be in your pool and you wouldn't know it?

EILEEN: No. It's in the backyard.

BRAD: Man, if I had a pool and found some-one in it, they'd be shot.

EILEEN: Well, we had a big deck. There's a deck and then the pool, so you couldn't really hear it.

CHERI: We used to do that. Didn't you ever go pool hopping?

WADE: No one had pools where I grew up.

BRAD: Plenty of people had pools around me, but we didn't swim in them.

CHERI: Man, we went all the time. In the middle of the night we'd go swim in some-one's pool.

BRAD: We didn't go swimming. We'd like catch a frog and throw it in their pool. Or we'd throw dye in there. You know, red dye pellets?

EILEEN: That's horrible.

BRAD: In fact, I was home for the weekend from college and we got caught. I didn't get caught, but there was this guy who didn't like this girl that we went to high school with. We were at a party and we're like, "Let's go mess a pool up." We rolled their yard . . . you know what that is?

EILEEN: What?

BRAD: We filled up the back seat and the hatch of this Iroc with toilet paper and rolled their yard, you know.

CHERI: How many people in your town drive Irocs?

BRAD: A lot. A lot. Anyway, she had this big old house and this big pool. Me and my friend Randy dropped off these guys Ragid and Mike. They were just rolling that yard and throwing the dye pellets, but this fam-ily had surveillance cameras in the yard. I remember we turned around in this place, C&S Builders. We started back there to pick them up, and all of a sudden all these Cor-nelia police come flying by and they screech up to the house and we just kept rolling on by. We were like, "Oh, man, they messed up." We turned around and came back and they were cuffed and gettin' put in the back of that police car.

WADE: Oh, no . . .

BRAD: I know, they got in all kinds of

trouble for that. They were in college.
You're too old to be doing that. When
you're in high school, you can get away
with it maybe. But you're in college,
they're gonna come down hard on you. I
mean, the bottom of the people's pool
wasn't cement. It was vinyl.

WADE: Wow, look at that. Congratulations,
gang, we are now in Los Angeles.

BRAD: I'm ready to put this dog to bed. I'm
ready to put this rooster to roost.

CHERI: I'm just the opposite. I'm sorry to
see it end. The second half of this trip has
gone by so fast.

BRAD: I'm ready to get home and get a phone
call from John Woo.

WADE: John Woo?

BRAD: He's the best action director that
ever lived. He did all of Bruce Lee's
movies and did Van Damme's last movie.

CHERI: Are you guys going to keep in
touch?

WADE: With everyone? Honestly?

CHERI: Of course.

WADE: I think we'll all go back to where we
live and probably call each other once in a
while . . . that will probably be about the
most of it. It's easy to say, "Oh, I'll
write and keep in touch." It's hard even
with your best friends. You say you'll keep
in touch, but it gets harder and harder and
then you're just back home.

BRAD: I'll agree with that. I'm busy
enough. I'll have memories, but that will
be it. I'm not gonna try to kid myself.

CHERI: I'm the type that everyone goes in

my phone book. I'm pretty good at keeping in touch. It may not be every month, but I'll just think of something sometimes and call . . . see what's happening . . . see if you marry what's-her-name.

BRAD: I doubt that's going to happen.

EILEEN: Wade, you'll probably be the first.

WADE: To get married? I'm willing to bet I won't be the first.

BRAD: I know I'm not going to be the first.

CHERI: I won't be.

WADE: I've said this before. People don't stop to realize that so much is going on around them. So many cultures and different places we've been and we don't realize in our everyday lives what goes on and what's out there. To think that there's people living in shacks. We just don't think about that. Or if we do, it's only for a moment.

CHERI: Or you look at the bad things happening around you and you forget about all these incredible things around us.

Everyone was beginning to have mixed emotions about the trip's end. It's been a long, long drive.

BRAD: Everybody talks about our generation being Generation X and how this world doesn't have a future or the future is dim. I think people in general are getting along a lot better now. I think if you just went back twenty years ago, you wouldn't have seen two whites, an Asian American, and an African American traveling cross-country together. That seems ironic. Twenty years ago, we would have all had more problems than we did.

WADE: We would all have had bad reactions to one another.

CHERI: We definitely wouldn't have been as welcome.

BRAD: When we were in the South, I still picked up a lot of prejudice. Y'all picked up on a couple of things, but people in general . . . there were things unsaid that I felt that you never saw. Until the older generation dies out, and we have the opportunity to take over. . .

WADE: Eileen's totally asleep. We should talk about her.

BRAD: What can you say about Eileen that she hasn't already said?

CHERI: Don't be mean, Brad. You're just jealous.

BRAD: I don't get jealous.

CHERI: She really came out of her shell after Dallas.

WADE: I know. What was that about? It was like someone woke her from the dead.

BRAD: She still doesn't tell you everything she's thinking, though.

CHERI: She's an innocent victim.

BRAD: Aw, she's no victim. She's nice. She's just quiet.

WADE: I think she was a little intimidated by the rest of us.

CHERI: She was intimidated by you guys. She's one of the easiest people to get along with. She has a lot of opinions on things, but I think the rest of us are more boisterous and just overpowered her. She put up with a couple of gang-bangs from the two of you guys that I was surprised she put up with.

BRAD: That'll make her a stronger person. You ain't gonna get no tears out of me for her.

They pull into the parking lot of their motel in Los Angeles.

CHERI: Eileen, wake up! We're done talking about you.

BRAD: Last stop, everybody out, end of the line, saddle up, ride off into the sunset, that's all folks!

Cheri, Brad, and Wade climb out of the car and start grabbing their luggage from the trunk.

Eileen wakes up and rubs her eyes. She's alone in the car.

EILEEN: Where are we?

FADE OUT.

DAY 20:

Friday, October 15:

Los Angeles, CA

TRAVEL: 0 miles.

PLACES OF INTEREST:
- **Hollywood Boulevard** is the gritty home to the town's history. Start at **Mann's Chinese Theater** at Hollywood Boulevard and La Brea Avenue. Stroll east to see such landmarks as **Musso** and **Frank's Grill** and **Fredrick's of Hollywood.**
- **Melrose Avenue** has been made famous by the television show. It's always been a funky strip of restaurants and fashion outlets. Start at Curson and walk east to Fairfax.
- For a cultural experience, drive to South Central Los Angeles and take a gander at the **Watts Towers.** Twisted spires of metal reach for the sky out of this blighted neighborhood. Imperial Highway at Wilmington Boulevard.
- **The Venice Beach Boardwalk** hosts Muscle Beach, countless street performers, awesome pick-up basketball, and freaks galore. Take Venice Boulevard to the beach. The boardwalk runs north to Rose Street.
- **The Garden of Oz,** a mosaic of plastic toys and campy trinkets imbedded in concrete, sits in the Hollywood Hills just beneath the Hollywood sign. Take Beachwood Drive into the hills. Turn left on Ledgewood Drive and find the garden on your right.
- **Olvera Street,** downtown, preserves the city's Latino heritage with shops, restaurants, and strolling mariachi musicians.
- **Griffith Park** is a cultural melting pot where you can ride horses, play golf, or visit the city zoo. It's also home to the Griffith Observatory, where the climax to *Rebel Without a Cause* was shot. The main entrance is on Los Feliz Boulevard, where it meets I-5.

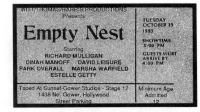

WITT/THOMAS/HARRIS PRODUCTIONS
Presents

Empty Nest

Starring
RICHARD MULLIGAN
DINAH MANOFF   DAVID LEISURE
PARK OVERALL   MARSHA WARFIELD
ESTELLE GETTY

TUESDAY
OCTOBER 19
1993

SHOWTIME
5:00 PM

GUESTS MUST
ARRIVE BY
4:00 PM

Taped At Sunset-Gower Studios - Stage 12
1438 No. Gower, Hollywood
Street Parking

Minimum Age
Admitted
12

Our first stop was Mann's Chinese Theater. As I looked at the stars on the "walk of fame" I thought of how for a month we've felt like stars. When people see the cameras, they think we're famous. The attention is fun.

PLACES TO EAT:
- **Pink's Hot Dogs** at the corner of La Brea Avenue and Melrose offers the best tubesteaks in the city, day or night. (213) 931-4223.
- **Canter's Deli** is where you'll spot celebrities out for a late-night nosh. 419 North Fairfax. (213) 651-2030.
- **Pacific Dining Car,** a comfortably elegant eatery built in 1921 around a railroad dining car, is open twenty-four hours and is famous for steaks. Downtown at 1310 West 6th Street. (213) 483-6000.
- **Roscoe's House of Chicken and Waffles** may sound like a gastrointestinal disaster, but there's a line out the door more often than not. 1518 North Gower Street. (213) 466-7453.
- For a serious power breakfast, try the pasta and eggs at **Hugo's Restaurant.** You'll be brushing elbows with producers, directors, agents, and the occasional celeb. 8401 Santa Monica Boulevard. (213) 654-3993.

Decided to drive through Beverly Hills and Rodeo Drive and ended up on the beach past Malibu. Sun was setting as we played in the water. Wade picked me up over his shoulder as if he were going to throw me in. I clenched my legs around him—if I was going, so was he! Surfers in the distance mooned us and yelled, "Film this!"

Ocean to ocean—the sun sank and the day ended.

Today was long—much free time— too much time—confusing feelings. Spent much of my time trying to figure out how I felt about things ... about Wade.

Wade pulled me aside before my interview. He turned off my microphone—you never know. Neither of us were very happy about how our relationship evolved. It had been difficult changing the terms of our relationship. The feelings were there, but we did our best to ignore them. Although I was flattered that he took me aside, I still wonder about his intentions—were they sincere, or was he merely manipulating me? Who knows? What does it matter now? I have bigger questions I should be pondering.

Afterward, the four of us watched a slide show of our trip. We laughed and drank and made fun of each other. For that brief hour we appeared to be best friends. It could have been a storybook ending to the trip, but I knew it wouldn't end that way. As soon as the show was over we had to say our good-byes and get Brad off to the airport. Tears immediately welled up in my eyes and I ran into the dressing room. Wade chased me down and hugged me. "Be happy," he repeated.

Anyway, we filmed the opening of the show. It should look really cool. Everything was dark, except for our faces. The camera swooped by as we spoke, creating an image of "nothingness" (if that makes sense).

Part 3

End of the Road

11/21

Jim Fitzgerald
St. Martin's Press
175 Fifth Avenue
New York, NY 10010

Dear Jim,

I can't believe more than a month has
passed since completing the trip. It's
taken that long to decompress. I don't
think any of us, cast or crew, had even an
inkling as to the intensity of this project. Aside from one day off in Dallas, we
ran just about twenty-four hours a day,
seven days a week. The atmosphere became
almost cultlike; a small group of intensely
devoted followers taking orders from a
charismatic leader, enduring sleep depri-
vation and endlessly repeated dogma. There
are few sights more disturbing than a
glassy-eyed production manager wandering
the walkways of a cheap motel at 2 A.M.,
barking call time at an exhausted crew. At
times I was just waiting for someone to
crack. One member of the team actually took
to sleepwalking and ventured stark naked
into the freezing Colorado night, calling
for his absent girlfriend. The schedule
took its toll on all relationships
involved, but we are beginning to regard
each other as normal human beings again.
Most of the crew has moved on to other proj-
ects. So it goes in Hollywood.

I spoke with Cheri the other day. She has
been keeping in touch with Brad and Eileen,
but Wade appears to be MIA. She is sending
me the journal she kept on the trip for
inclusion in the book. Eileen is soon off
to Europe where she will spend her next

semester studying abroad. Brad has taken a job with the Georgia State Patrol. Cheri broke up with her boyfriend and seems apathetic toward the dating scene in St. Louis. She mentioned that she's thinking of moving to Los Angeles.

Kurt and J.D. are editing the show in Denver and indicate favorable results. We came away with more than two hundred hours of raw footage. Imagine the task of cutting that into a fifty-two-minute special. It's nearly as overwhelming as the production itself. Interesting, the condensation process: months of planning and preparation and three full weeks of shooting for fifty-two minutes of crystallized material that will be broadcast, and then exist mainly as a flicker or two of memory.

At any rate, I'm gearing up to compile the material for the book. As they finish with tapes in Denver, I'll begin transcribing.

Yours,

Andrew Hoegl
Freewheelin' Films/Slam Dunk Productions

Suggested Reading

for More Fun on the Road

Bergheim, Laura A. *Weird Wonderful America: The Nation's Most Offbeat and Off-the-Beaten-Path Tourist Attractions.* New York: Collier Books, 1988.

Brinkley, Douglas. *The Magic Bus: An American Odyssey.* New York: Harcourt Brace & Company, 1993.

Coupland, Douglas. *Generation X: Tales for an Accelerated Culture.* New York: St. Martin's Press, 1991.

Davis, Mary Dymond. *Going off the Beaten Path: An Untraditional Travel Guide to the U.S.* Chicago: The Noble Press, Inc., 1991.

Myers, Arthur. *The Ghostly Gazetteer: America's Most Fascinating Haunted Landmarks.* Chicago: Contemporary Books, 1990.

Staten, Vince. *Unauthorized America: A Travel Guide to the Places the Chamber of Commerce Won't Tell You About.* New York: Harper and Row, 1990.

Stern, Jane, and Michael Stern. *Roadfood.* New York: Harper Perennial, 1992.

Tiller, Veronica E., ed. *Discover Indian Reservations USA: A Visitors' Welcome Guide.* Denver: Council Publications, 1992.

Wallis, Michael. *Route 66: The Mother Road.* New York: St. Martin's Press, 1990.

Wilkins, Mike, Ken Smith, and Doug Kirby. *The New Roadside America: The Modern Traveler's Guide to the Wild and Wonderful World of America's Tourist Attractions.* New York: Fireside, 1992.